The Cosmopolites
The Coming of
the Global Citizen

COLUMBIA GLOBAL REPORTS
NEW YORK

The Cosmopolites
The Coming of
the Global Citizen

Atossa Araxia
Abrahamian

Canada

United
States

London,
Ontario

St. Kitts
and Nevis

Antigua
and Barbuda

The Cosmopolites: The Coming of the Global Citizen
Copyright © 2015 by Atossa Araxia Abrahamian
All rights reserved

Published by Columbia Global Reports
91 Claremont Avenue, Suite 515, New York, NY 10027
www.globalreports.columbia.edu
facebook.com/columbiaglobalreports
@columbiaGR

Library of Congress Control Number: 2015946813
ISBN: 978-0-9909763-6-3

Book design by Strick&Williams
Map design by Jeffrey L. Ward
Author photograph by Victor Jeffreys II

Printed in the United States of America

CONTENTS

Foreword

So many stories begin with borders.

I was brought up with no sense of a motherland or father-
land, no pledges of allegiance, no flags with which I identified.
I'm a citizen of Switzerland, where I was raised; Canada, where I
was born while my mother was on vacation; and Iran, where my
parents of Russian and Armenian descent lived before leaving
to study in Europe. I speak fluent French, bad German, and
passable Russian; I travel as much as I can; and I have spent
most of my life thus far attending international schools and
universities, most recently in New York City, where I've lived
for the greater part of the past decade. Most of the people I grew
up around were United Nations employees and their families.
Everyone, it seemed, was international. So the notion of belonging not to a particular country or community, but to the greater
world, was an intuitive one to me. Every holiday season at my
Geneva elementary school, we were even coached to dress up

in various national costumes and sing "We Are the World" for
our beaming, multicultural families. During my first such per-
formance, when I was four years old, I had a meltdown because I
couldn't tell my teacher what country's garb to dress me in.

I recognize my blind inheritance of an international
upbringing, of bumping into acquaintances at airports, of
always having someone to call on during an unexpected layover.
But this condition comes with some challenges, both personal
and political. The historian Tony Judt wrote that the Palestinian
theorist Edward Said

> tellingly observed just a few months before his death, "I still
> have not been able to understand what it means to love a
> country." That, of course, is the characteristic condition of
> the rootless cosmopolitan. It is not very comfortable or safe
> to be without a country to love: It can bring down upon your
> head the anxious hostility of those for whom such rootless-
> ness suggests a corrosive independence of spirit. But it is
> liberating: The world you look out upon may not be as reas-
> suring as the vista enjoyed by patriots and nationalists, but
> you see further. As Said wrote in 1993, "I have no patience
> with the position that 'we' should only or mainly be con-
> cerned with what is 'ours.'"

This discomfort with the national "we" is one that I—and,
as I've learned, countless others—share with him, regardless of
our origins. Increasingly, ours is a world of stateless natives and
citizen-strangers; of undocumented immigrants who know no
land other than the one that rejects them; of men and women of
the world with no fixed place to call home. More than ever, people

10   want or need to belong to, or be accepted in, places they were not
assigned to by the accident of birth, whether for economic, personal, or political reasons: the farm worker from Mexico who
looks to California for seasonal employment; the boats of Syrian
refugees who drown escaping violence on their way to Europe;
the Chinese billionaire who invests in foreign stocks and educates
his kids in Canada; the Irishman in love with a Singaporean girl,
kept apart because of artificial borders set by historical accident.

The cosmopolitan idea that Edward Said embodied is itself
a kind of historical accident. It emerged in the West after the
Peloponnesian War—ostensibly a defeat for Athens, but, more
importantly, a fatal blow to the international order over which
the city-state had presided. In the following century, Greece's
best political minds set themselves to picking up the pieces.
Lamenting the incompetence of democracy, Plato imagined
a city-state ruled by philosopher-kings, and his star student,
Aristotle, surveyed hundreds of cities and proposed a mixed
constitution combining the best elements of each. But as
Greece's city-states languished and new powers arose, these
proposed fixes seemed ever more out of date. The golden age of
the *polis* wasn't coming back.

Into this intellectual clearing stepped a man in a barrel.
Diogenes of Sinope was the West's first conscientious objector,
a man who thought the customs and rules of the city, any city,
had rotted beyond hope. The lifestyle he chose—drinking and
debating all day, urinating openly, sleeping in a wine-barrel—
won him the nickname of *kunos*, the dog. His school took up the
label proudly, calling themselves Cynics, and when respectable

people asked Diogenes what city was his home, he replied, "I am a *kosmopolites*": a citizen of the universe.

Diogenes did not come to reinvent politics but to end them. As the classicist Melissa Lane explains, "Diogenes declared himself a *kosmopolites* as a way of declaring himself to be no *polites*, no citizen, at all." This rejection of all politics and politicians was as seductive then as it is today: When Alexander the Great offered a naked, sun-bathing Diogenes any favor he desired, he asked only that the young prince quit blocking the sun.

The Cynics were not the only, or even the most influential, promoters of the new cosmopolitan idea. A generation after Diogenes, a young intellectual firebrand named Zeno of Citium set up shop in the very heart of Athens, in a strip-mall colonnade called the Stoa. The school he founded, known as the Stoics, would be the most influential source of ideas for the next ten centuries in the West. They disagreed with Plato and Aristotle and agreed with the Cynics that the city-state was over; but whereas Diogenes had tossed citizenship to the merry dirt, the Stoics exalted it. All men on earth, they contended, share in the *logos*, the divine reason of the gods. The world must be governed not by local custom but by the reason that unites all mankind and binds together the universe. And thus, in versions high and low, transcendent and cynical, the cosmopolitan idea came to be.

The Romans put these Greek ideas into practice, and their vast empire was sustained on the notion of universal order and natural law that the Stoics had propounded. Even after antiquity ended and the "world city" ceased to rule an empire, Latin

12   language, Christian church, and Roman legal codes were the essential common currency of the West. Only when the rupture in Christian unity led to another total war between Catholics and Protestants in the sixteenth century did the space open for a new organizing principle: a system of sovereign nation-states, embodied most famously in the Treaty of Westphalia in 1648. The Westphalian system is, for better or worse, the one in which we all live—the one which issues passports and grants equal sovereign rights to France and Kuwait and the Comoro Islands. Since 1945 it has kept the world's chief powers from another total war. But as history shows, the nation-state system was neither humanity's first conception of citizenship, nor will it be the last.

I'd been thinking a lot about what it meant to be a citizen of anywhere when, just weeks after graduating from journalism school, I learned that I'd won the U.S. Diversity Visa lottery, also known as the Green Card lottery, which would fast-track me into permanent resident status in the United States. The lottery's premise is to give citizens of underrepresented nations a chance to come to America and contribute to the diversity that this nation prides itself on. I'd applied as a Swiss national. Like many international students in the U.S., I'd been struggling for years to obtain a work visa so I could remain in New York. When I found out that I had won, the news seemed too good to be true.

It was—my application was ultimately disqualified. The U.S. government did not consider me a Swiss native because I wasn't born there. That rendered my whole application, and the draw of the winning ticket, invalid. But my disqualification also hinted at a larger, structural quandary: Why, in the twenty-first century, are people still categorized by where they're born? Why do nations have the last word in determining our identities? What of all these rumors declaring the world flat, and the nation-state passé?

A few months later, I received an email from A Small World inviting me to a "Global Citizenship" conference. A Small World is a social network for the private-jet set, the kind of website where Italian bankers living in Singapore debate the merits of the latest Gulfstream and the pitfalls of intercontinental dating. I wrote the site off as a mildly odious gimmick and gave it little thought until this particular email evaded my spam filter and made its way into my inbox on a slow workday afternoon.

It was the term "global citizenship" in the subject line that caught my interest. Thinking that the conference would confront my questions, or at least float a coherent vision of what it meant to be global, I clicked through to the link, opened the webpage, and started reading. What I found was hardly a soul-searching philosophical enterprise. The global citizenship conference, it turned out, was a trade event on how to buy, sell, and renounce national citizenship—completely legally, and above board—in order to travel more freely, pay lower taxes, hide from their governments, and overall, buy a plan B in case of trouble back home. Adding to the intrigue was the fact that this business appeared to be mediated by a small handful of privately held companies that helped poor countries like St. Kitts and Nevis and Dominica sell their citizenship to the wealthy from Russia, China, and the Middle East. One of these companies was using A Small World to reach their target demographic.

14   The characters I met at the conference fascinated me: the Swiss passport impresario, preaching the gospel of global citizenship to a crowd of buttoned-up tax lawyers; the ex-American with five passports who lived on The World, a cruise ship that circles the globe, taking its denizens all over the high seas; the tall, red-bearded chairman of A Small World who'd gone to boarding school with some friends of mine in the Swiss Alps and was now traveling the world pitching St. Kitts as a trendy location to buy a second passport. It's not surprising that some of these go-betweens are known locally as "pirates of the Caribbean."

     The biggest triumph of the modern nation-state has been to convince large groups of people that a status conferred to them arbitrarily upon birth was, in fact, *not* for sale, and indeed, worth defending unto death. "Regardless of the actual inequality and exploitation that may prevail in each, the nation is always conceived as a deep, horizontal comradeship," the political scientist Benedict Anderson wrote in his important 1983 book *Imagined Communities*. "Ultimately it is this fraternity that makes it possible, over the past two centuries, for so many millions of people, not so much to kill, as willingly to die for such limited imaginings." But the conference suggested that comradeship had given way to commerce, and that citizenship—both national and global—was becoming a luxury convenience to be bought and sold. The physical and emotional distance I felt from "my" countries is not unique; like ships flying flags of convenience, more people carry nationalities of convenience, and a growing number of countries have stepped up to accommodate them.

Citizenship in the twenty-first century is changing, change-able, interchangeable; new crises explode the old mythologies of national power and take personal allegiances with them. A 2015 Politico story detailed how British citizens, fearing their country's exit from the European Union, were scrambling to apply for citizenship of other European nations so that they could keep on living and working in Brussels. "In a worst-case scenario, I'm going to have marry [*sic*] my partner of the last twenty years, because she's got an Irish passport," one Brit told Politico Europe. "In a slightly less worst-case-scenario, I have to become Belgian, which I actually wouldn't mind doing. I'd quite like to be Belgian." (Romance, at least, still knows no borders.)

The definition of global citizenship that I learned about while attending passport-selling events was one that applies to a very small number of people—not the 1 percent, but the 0.1 percent. A St. Kitts passport could be mine for $250,000. But after immersing myself in the world of high-end passport brokers, I had a feeling that the story of twenty-first-century citizenship was bigger than a few billionaires seeking their next passport.

That feeling turned out to be rooted in fact: In a conversation with a friend in Dubai, I learned that the government of the United Arab Emirates had launched a novel program to grant citizenship to the *bidoon*—stateless residents of the UAE who had no documentation, and whom the country considered ille-gal immigrants. Only the Gulf monarchy didn't give the *bidoon* Emirati citizenship; it bought for them citizenship from the Comoro Islands—an impoverished archipelago off the east

16   coast of Africa whose very name most of these would-be citizens wouldn't recognize. The agreement the Gulf state had with the Comoros did not include a provision to actually resettle them on the islands. Their Comorian citizenship would be, by design, paper-thin.

What kind of citizenship was this? Who had come up with such a plan? How much money was exchanging hands, and how did the *bidoon* feel about suddenly "becoming" Comorian? The story seemed to indicate that spillover effects of the high-end passport market were a lot more widespread than helping the wealthy expatriate. It suggested that repressive governments had identified a market-based solution to citizenship as a valid way to manipulate a second-class population. This, too, was confirmed: I later learned that one of the recipients of this citizenship had been deported to Thailand for speaking out against the authorities. I tracked the man down in London, Ontario, where he'd sought refugee status. After spending his entire life as a stateless non-citizen of the Emirates, he, too, had become a global citizen—albeit an unwitting one.

The "global citizens" who buy papers from Caribbean tax havens without setting foot in their adopted countries, and the disenfranchised residents of the Emirates who obtain Comorian citizenship with no plans to ever go there, represent two sides of a common phenomenon. They challenge any meaningful connection between man and state. Global citizenship is itself a new form of statelessness.

This book is a product of this sense of statelessness, of being somehow "of" the world without belonging anywhere within it. What does citizenship become when it becomes

detached from any kind of civic engagement and political identification—when it is a matter of convenience, not community?
What are the stakes when members of a community no longer
feel a particular kinship or loyalty to any particular place? What
does it mean when the wealthy can move freely between countries and exploit the "borderless" world that globalization has
promised, but that the poor who try to cross borders can't—or,
if they can, routinely die trying?

Who among us gets to be "global"? I think the stories in this
book begin to give an answer.

Prologue

On October 10, 2008, eleven officials from the Comoro Islands made their way from their respective villages to a spare one-terminal airport not far from the capital, where, on a runway overlooking the Indian Ocean, a private plane stood waiting to fly them to Kuwait. The road that led them there was one of the archipelago nation's longest—a twenty-kilometer stretch that skims the corniche up and down the west side of the island, lined with pineapple, breadfruit, and mango trees, but also potholes and piles of trash. The Comoros supply the world with ylang-ylang, a flower used to produce high-end perfumes, and along the airport road, the country's pungent flora, combined with its lack of a functional waste-collection system and its tropical climate, create a unique olfactory experience: one part hot garbage, the other Chanel No. 5.

That balmy day, on the other side of the world, central bankers were scrambling to prop up the global economy as the

Dow Jones industrial average suffered its worst week ever. The   19
Comorian representatives on their way to the airport had money
on their minds, too, but not the abstract kind that shows up on
tickers and balance sheets. Their country was completely broke,
and had been that way for as long as they could remember. The
Comoros' annual gross domestic product per capita was $740
that year, with economic growth at just 0.8 percent for 2007.
The country was negotiating with the International Monetary
Fund and the World Bank to qualify for debt relief under a program designed to help the poorest countries; 45 percent of the
population lived below the poverty line. Still today, infrastructure is abysmal; running water is a rarity. Even the Comorian
parliamentary building lacks the most basic amenities. When
politicians complain that they have no power, they mean it literally. Electricity, in the rooms that are equipped with it, only runs
for several hours at a time, and that's on a good day; overall, only
60 percent of residents in Grande Comore, the biggest island,
have access to electricity at all. In Anjouan, the middle island,
it's closer to 50 percent; in the smallest, Moheli, only 20 percent
of people can turn the lights on at night.

The reason behind the trip to Kuwait was economic. Earlier
that year, the Comorian government had received a proposal
from some visiting Arab businessmen. What if the Comoros
started to sell their citizenship to raise funds?

There was a great demand for passports in the Middle
East, the men explained, both from wealthy individuals seeking a second or third nationality to make traveling and working abroad easier, and from the *bidoon*—Arabic for "without,"
a name for people who have been denied citizenship from the

20   start. Some countries in the region were even willing to pay good
money to procure Comorian citizenship in bulk for the *bidoon*,
the businessmen claimed. All the Comorians would have to do
was pass a law allowing for this type of transaction, and print
some passports.

The Comorian president at the time, Ahmed Abdallah
Sambi, and his vice president, Idi Nadhoim, were intrigued. This
was money they could use to fix the roads, take out the trash, buy
fuel, and build desperately needed infrastructure. Such a des-
titute country could not afford to be high-minded about a few
pieces of paper. Beggar states cannot be chooser states.

The parliamentarians didn't see it that way. The offer, they
said, was a Faustian bargain. Wasn't selling citizenship to complete strangers, in some way, selling a piece of their country's
soul? They rejected a proposed "economic citizenship" bill in a
heated session in July, contending that it would be tantamount
to auctioning off their nationality.

Two months later, the Arab businessmen offered to put
together a "fact-finding mission" to the Gulf states, all expenses
paid. Conveniently, the trip was scheduled to take place ahead
of the next session of Parliament. Six of the law's most vocal
opponents were invited.

Ibrahim M'houmadi Sidi, the sad-eyed vice president of
Parliament at the time, led the delegation. A master of rehearsed
earnestness, Sidi, who now teaches at the local university, was
then a committed member of the opposition. He lived in a run-
down house with a tin roof in the center of the capital, Moroni,
with his wife and baby; his car, parked outside his home, was
broken, and he hadn't had the means to repair it.

Aboubacar Said Salim, the secretary-general of Parliament, was another delegate who'd agreed to take the trip in spite of his initial disgust for the entire project. A self-styled public intellectual, Salim lost his most recent novel to a computer malfunction. He saw the trip as a sort of civic duty, and he was ready to absorb all the information he could and report back.

Abdou Mouminé, the president of the Parliamentary finance commission, went along, he says, because he believed in opening up the Comoros to the rest of the world and inviting foreigners to invest. How they did so mattered very little in his eyes. "Here in our country, we have a ticking time bomb," he told me. "We have a university that churns out unemployed young people, and over the years, if these young Comorians don't find work, it's going to explode."

Houssamou Mohamed Madi was one of three representatives on the junket who did not hold a parliamentary position at the time; he was hired as a translator, since he speaks both Arabic and French. Most recently employed by the Ministry of Justice, he is a nervous man, easily intimidated, prone to sweating profusely and stammering under pressure. He had wanted to publicize the trip, but his higher-ups said no. "They thought that the fact that many people would be obtaining nationality might arouse controversy," he recalled one stormy evening last November in his office, while trying his best to stop the leaking ceiling from causing a small flood.

Also present was Said Mohamed Sagaf, a dignified older gentleman who'd served for a year as the minister of foreign affairs and would go on to take several such voyages with a group called the Kuwait-Comoros Friendship Association.

22   "[The businessmen] had made so much noise about the proposal," said Sagaf. "They dangled all sorts of promises in front of us. We wanted to see for ourselves."

The men did not have to wait in line for hours to check their bags, as is customary at the airport, even when there are only a dozen people in the queue, even with four people working the counter. They didn't have to sweat through security or passport control, swatting the large ants that have taken up residence in the airport's grimy corners off their arms and legs. They simply boarded the plane, made themselves comfortable, and took off. It was amazing, what money could do.

As the plane climbed higher, the men caught an aerial view of their country, its hilly slopes swollen with green breadfruits that grow year-round in the fertile volcanic soil. A pale ring of sand, flecked with ash-black rocks, surrounded the island; at the center was Mount Karthala, one of the world's largest active volcanoes.

Comoros fits the cliché of an island paradise from above—every bit as pretty as neighboring Mauritius, Réunion, or the Seychelles, which between them attract hundreds of thousands of tourists a year. And yet on the ground this natural beauty has gotten Comoros nowhere. Most people haven't heard of it; those who have can't quite believe that it is a sovereign nation at all. The country's most distinguishing feature is a series of around twenty post-independence coups d'état often perpetrated by foreign mercenaries. The islands' nickname in international circles is "Cloud Coup-Coup land." What is it about Comoros that's made it consistently rank among the poorest nations in the world? What, the men wondered, were they doing wrong?

Islands of the Moon

The plane began its descent toward Kuwait City some six hours later, its passengers well fed and well rested thanks to a smooth ride and impeccable in-flight service. The landscape going down was a dramatic change from their homeland—an arid grid of flat buildings, with the occasional skyscraper asserting its presence, steel and glass exteriors glimmering. In the distance, oilfields, big black refinery towers, the Persian Gulf, and miles of sand stretched as far as the eye could see.

When the men disembarked, they were welcomed by a tall, bald man with a firm handshake and a Colgate smile. His Western clothes caused him to stand out from the Kuwaitis in traditional white robes and headdresses. He greeted the Comorians in perfect French. They needed no introductions. The man was a figure of such prominence in Moroni that his name hangs under the breath of loiterers on street corners, whispered between secretaries in government buildings, and cursed by taxi drivers on the bumpy roads.

26   His name is Bashar Kiwan, a Kuwait City-based Syrian-French media executive and erstwhile honorary consul of Comoros to Kuwait. It was his team that had brought the economic citizenship proposal to President Sambi, and in the past months he and his associates—mostly young Syrian and Lebanese men—had become fixtures on Moroni's small social scene, with their shining sport utility vehicles, imported Middle Eastern buffets, flashy watches, and gaudy polos. Kiwan himself would visit about once a month, coming and going from government buildings as he pleased and throwing parties at the upscale (by local standards) Itsandra Beach Hotel, which his company would later manage.

That Kiwan and the average Comorian live under the same moon and stars that glow in the Moroni night is a testament to how unevenly the global economy distributes its gifts. The Comorians are orphans of a bygone era, alone, afraid, and adrift; Kiwan is a son of globalization, a free agent, a man without a country. Born in Kuwait to Syrian parents and educated in Montpelier in the south of France, Kiwan is bi-national and trilingual—he speaks Arabic, French, and English—and highly proficient in the additional business lexicon of "disruptions," "impacts," and "innovations."

Before Kiwan went into business in the Comoros, he'd made his fortune with Al Waseet International, a tangle of media and advertising companies currently operating across the Middle East and Eastern Europe. He started publishing his first classified advertising newspaper in Kuwait in the early 1990s with just $5,000 in capital, according to company lore. Al Waseet—Arabic for "the mediator"—now employs more than

5,000 people in a dozen countries, winning Kiwan, its chairman, comparisons in a German magazine to Rupert Murdoch, and a sharklike reputation to match.

Kiwan's charisma and business savvy had served him well over the years. He didn't just make friends with powerful people; he went into business with them. An early associate was Sheikh Sabah Jaber Mubarak al Sabah, the son of the current Kuwaiti prime minister and Kiwan's jumper cable to high society. Sabah served on the board of Al Waseet and backed a number of Kiwan ventures; the alliance gave Kiwan instant credibility. "It was Bashar's guarantor—his moral collateral," says Mansur Muhtar, an old friend of Kiwan's in the Comoros. "It meant he could approach investors in the Comoros and elsewhere and say he was working with the Kuwaiti government."

In Syria, his longtime business partner is Majd Suleiman, the son of the former Syrian security chief Bahjat Suleiman and, according to a U.S. congressional research service paper, a member of Syrian President Bashar al-Assad's inner circle. Kiwan and Suleiman founded the United Group, a publicly traded Syrian media company that publishes titles sympathetic to the Assad regime and was affiliated with Al Waseet International. Kiwan then became the president of a Kuwait-based trade group called the Syrian Business Council, which allowed him to forge close ties with global business executives and international dignitaries when they came to visit. His charm was both pleasant and highly effective. "When you met him, you'd have your ideas, but after you spoke to him you'd leave with his ideas because he was so convincing," Muhtar says. "He really knows how to sell his projects."

28   Kiwan lived in the exclusive Messila neighborhood of Kuwait City. He was married to Angélique, a gorgeous French-woman whom he met on a ski trip in college, and the couple had one son, Jad.

Still, on the eve of his forty-third birthday, Kiwan had hit what might be described as a sand ceiling. Kiwan was an expat living in Kuwait, and he didn't want to become a naturalized citizen. The country's draconian citizenship laws, which made naturalization close to impossible, and even then distinguished between native-born and "new" Kuwaitis, denying the latter the right to vote and rendering them subject to denaturalization at the government's whims.

There were privileges that he simply wasn't born with and that hard work, ambition, and entrepreneurialism couldn't provide. Sure, he could influence some of the biggest names in Kuwait; but he could only run the show to a limited degree, and usually from the sidelines.

There were no such rules in the Comoros.

To begin to grasp the appeal of the Comoros to a power-hungry foreigner, and to comprehend the islands' receptiveness to the designs of these ambitious outsiders, consider the legacy of the mercenary Bob Denard, the man believed to have inspired Frederick Forsyth's novel *Dogs of War*. Denard, born Gilbert Bourgeaud in Bordeaux, France, in 1929, was an officer in the French army whose aversion to communism and appetite for adventure had led him to participate in numerous battles across the African continent as a hired gun. He fought in or led post-colonial insurrections in Katanga, Rhodesia, Gabon, Yemen,

Benin, Zaire, and Angola, claiming to have been supported, albeit tacitly, by the French government. Denard would compare his work to that of the corsairs, the privateers who would raid rival ships during monarchic times. "The corsairs in France would receive written permission from the king to attack foreign ships," he would say. "I didn't have such permission, but I had passports given to me by the intelligence services."

Denard's Comorian adventures began in 1975, when the mercenary was living in Paris and itching to wield his mortars once more. He was pushing fifty, and the lawless environments he was used to operating in were becoming few and far between; he sorely missed the adventurer's life.

Then, one day, Denard received a phone call from an acquaintance of his in Geneva, Switzerland. The Comoro Islands, the man on the line explained, had a problem: they'd recently gained independence from France but their first president, Ahmed Abdallah, had lasted barely a month in power before a young socialist named Ali Soilih deposed him and sent him away to Anjouan. One of Soilih's allies wanted Denard to help get rid of Abdallah for good. Could he help?

Denard, bored out of his mind, jumped at the chance, and off to the Comoros he went. What awaited him was almost total chaos—and an opportunity to seize power in a way he never had before. Thanks to centuries of poverty, political instability, and colonization, the Union of the Comoros has almost no political identity to speak of. It is one country; it could just as easily be three countries, or no country at all. Iain Walker, a researcher at Oxford University, wrote a paper called "What Came First, the Nation or the State? Political Process in the Comoro Islands."

30   His conclusion: "There is, in no real sense, either state or nation
in the Comoros."

Even today, the Comoro Islands are a lost place—too small to
make out on a map, too poor to wield any geopolitical influence,
too distant to register as a real country to anyone who doesn't
study the region. The Arabic word for Comoros is *Kamar*, or
"moon"—a name that speaks to the islands' breathtaking night
sky, and the uncanny feeling of total remove that many outsiders experience when they visit. It's unclear who its first settlers
were, though it's believed that the islands were first inhabited
by Malayo-Polynesians in the fourth and fifth centuries, then
colonized by Africans in the eighth. Since the fifteenth century,
the islands have seen a heavy Arab influence, thanks in large
part to the Shirazi sultans who controlled several city-states on
the African coast and moved to the islands, bringing Islam with
them. Then, in 1841, the French took possession of Mayotte,
and in the ensuing decades claimed the rest of the islands, which
remained under colonial rule until 1912, when they were classified as a province of Madagascar.

After World War II, the Comoros were "freed" from
Madagascar to become a self-standing French overseas territory. Over the following decades, plans were made for the
islands to become independent. Then, for the first and most
likely last time in Comorian history, local leaders decided to
work ahead of schedule, and called for national elections early,
without informing the French. Overnight, in 1975, Ahmed
Abdallah became the country's first independent ruler.

The Comoros as we now know them were thus born—but
they emerged from the colonial womb a limb short. Voters in the

fourth Comoro island, Mayotte, abstained from the independence vote, opting to remain under French control. Anger over the island's decision (and a perceived French conspiracy) still sends locals into a tizzy: On the road to the Moroni port, a large sign declares that *Mayotte est Comorienne, et le sera a jamais*—"Mayotte is Comorian, and will be so forever."

Denard did not concern himself with local politics; he was there to do one job. He arrived in Anjouan in a plane packed with rifles and a scrappy army of Comorian men. With their help, sent Abdallah packing to Paris. There was only one casualty: a relative of Soilih's who was accidentally decapitated by a machete.

Denard was back in business—only propping up Soilih turned out to be a mistake. The new president's hard-partying lifestyle made him an unpopular leader in the overwhelmingly Muslim Comoros, and within a couple of years, the country was flailing. Abdallah, the ex-president still in exile in Paris, felt a lingering responsibility to help. So he called on the only person he knew who could shake things up: Denard, the very man who had precipitated his own exile.

The job, to be fair, wasn't a hard one. Denard and some fellow mercenaries from Europe pulled up to Grand Comore in a deep-sea trawler. They posed as scientists on a research trip; they had a black German shepherd and a literal boatload of weapons in tow. As the legend goes, Denard caught Soilih drunk in bed with two young girls on May 13, 1978, and hauled him off to prison, where, 16 days later, he was shot and killed. Abdallah regained power, and Denard was rewarded with a privileged position as the head of his Presidential Guard for the next eleven years.

32   "I realize that what attracts [us mercenaries] to the Indian Ocean," Denard wrote in his diaries, "is participating in the creation of a new country." Walter Bruyere-Ostells, a lecturer in history at Sciences Po Aix who wrote a 2014 book on Denard, says Denard "perceived himself as a new Bonaparte arriving in Egypt." Ostells also notes that since Denard's day, the Comorians have accepted the continued presence of foreign strongmen in their country almost as a matter of course.

Denard provided security for the president, bringing in recruits and training them in the ways of the hired gun. But he also took an interest in leading development initiatives. He rallied his men to build a rainwater collection facility and encouraged them to train locals to run the mechanized farm he'd set up. The vehicle for his business activities was the Presidential Guard itself, a setup comparable to the Revolutionary Guard in Iran, which has political, public, and commercial arms. When South Africa found itself under international scrutiny in the 1980s, the Presidential Guard, under Denard's watch, positioned the Comoros as an offshore center for South Africans to bypass apartheid-era sanctions. The South Africans would finance Denard's mercenary unit and funnel their money through the Comoros, effectively laundering it and allowing them to carry on business as usual, sanctions be damned.

Denard grew attached to his new home. He told French television at the time that he had "the intention of establishing myself definitively here as a full Comorian." He changed his name to Saïd Mustapha Mahdjoub and converted to Islam. (This man of many names had previously converted to Judaism, and was ultimately put to rest in a Catholic graveyard.) Denard took Comorian wives, and fathered children with a total of seven women there.

What was missing between Denard and the Comorians, though, was trust—once a mercenary, always a mercenary. Denard's men, many of them white Europeans who espoused virulent right-wing ideologies, acted like they owned the place. "It got to the point where you'd go into a store and they'd skip the line and get served first," a local told French journalists who were shooting a documentary on Denard.

Abdallah sensed trouble brewing, and in 1989 the president signed a secret decree ordering the disarmament of the mercenary army. Hours later, he died of a gunshot wound following a mysterious altercation in his office, at which Denard himself was present. He claimed he was not guilty of the shooting and, on the order of an influential French businessman, was taken to South Africa by French paratroopers. He was extradited to France shortly thereafter to face trial for Abdallah's murder, but the charges were dropped, and he was acquitted.

With his departure, Comoros began a slow but steady turn away from France and toward their Muslim brothers in the Gulf states. It wasn't easy. In Denard's heyday, Iain Walker remembers, "there was money—things were run by proxy by the French and South Africans."

"Things actually worked, the roads were paved," he told me. "Today it's not functioning quite as smoothly."

Denard did not return to the islands until 1995, when, homesick and pledging to restore order, he threatened to depose yet another president, Said Mohamed Djohar. His team was markedly smaller: He had just thirty men with him, and they

34 floated in on inflatable dinghies. This time, the French thwarted his takeover by intervening, arresting him, and sending him back to France for good to face the law. Most of the charges against him—the murder of Abdallah, for instance, and the attempted overthrow of the Djohar govenment—were dropped on lack of evidence or abandoned when he died in 2007.

Denard's adventure in the archipelago serves as a cautionary tale: Comoros is a country of men, not laws. You can bend, break, and burn all the rules you want—as long as the man of the hour stands behind you.

Bashar Kiwan's love affair with the Comoro Islands began the year after Denard's final flop of an insurrection, when he traveled as part of a delegation of businessmen seeking their luck where no competitors dared tread. "I discovered a virgin country that was coming out of a little civil war with some mercenaries," Kiwan told me in late 2014. "It was just like heaven." But the decade after Denard's departure was a tumultuous one rife with political unrest, and given that the country's entire constitution was liable to change from one day to the next, it was far too risky for even the most intrepid businessman—at least, an unarmed one.

It wasn't until 2005 that then-president Azali Assoumani invited the Gulf businessmen to come back and pick up where they left off. This time, Kiwan sensed an opportunity. He came back again, then again, and again, until his visits became a monthly occurrence. He introduced prominent figures in the Gulf to their Comorian counterparts, ingratiating himself to the islands' small business elite, and making inquiries about banking licenses, telecom licenses, aviation licenses, and infrastructure contracts. He signed a memorandum of understanding with the Comorian authorities for the establishment of some ambitious projects, including the country's first commercial bank.

"Bashar felt that he could have a significant influence on the country," says a senior manager of Kiwan's holding company who lived and worked in Moroni for four years. "Having a direct line to the President and his government was what was most important to Bashar. He couldn't do that in other countries; he felt important there, and that's why he liked it. I had the same feeling myself."

According to local lawmakers, Kiwan was always talking about Sheikh Sabah. This pleased the Comorians, because Sabah belongs to the Kuwaiti ruling family. The Comorians thought of Kiwan's associate as a bona fide prince. "Theoretically, a prince is a credible person who deals with many countries, so I told myself that if he could work with the Western countries, we couldn't reproach him for anything and that we should let him do business here," ex-president Azali Assoumani told me. "Princes are highly cultured people! He was very young, very sympathetic, very elegant and extremely intelligent. I only met him twice, but I saw in him a man who was serious and who wanted to work hard."

Kiwan then scoped out presidential hopefuls for an ally on the 2006 ballot, and found his man in Ahmed Abdallah Mohamed Sambi, an idealistic imam-turned-mattress-and-perfume salesman and a relative newcomer to politics. To an opportunistic outsider, Sambi's political malleability must have plainly beamed from his face. But to the common Comorian citizen, Sambi seemed like the leader the islands had been waiting for. He seemed honest, a hard worker who still lived above his modest mattress shop—no risk of Soilih-esque debauchery. Sambi came from Anjouan, an island whose residents harbor some secessionist tendencies, but he spoke of peace, cooperation, and national unity. He was a religious man who'd studied Islamic political theory in Qom, Iran, but expressed no interest in turning the islands into a theocracy. It was an appealing stance for a population whose brand of Islam is best characterized as "slacker Sunni." "I am not ashamed to be a Muslim but our country is not ready to be an Islamic state," he told the BBC. "I will not make anyone wear the veil." He nevertheless became known as "The Ayatollah."

By all accounts, even those of his fiercest detractors, Sambi was also devastatingly charismatic. Fair-skinned with a glowing bronze complexion and a beatific calm, he looked—and, observers in Comorian political circles say, considered himself—more like a prophet than a politician. He dressed the part, too, favoring turbans of brilliant green silk and ivory robes with gold embroidery over the stiff white tunics and fez-like brown caps that Comorian men traditionally wear. In addition to fluent French and the local patois, he spoke a lyrical, poetic Arabic that made speeches about state budgets sound like scripture—a talent no doubt picked up during his stint in Qom. "He was a political animal," says a development professional who met regularly with Sambi and saw him speak on numerous occasions. "When he walked into the room, you stopped and stared. When he talked, you wanted to believe his every word."

"When you convince a population living in misery that by some miracle you're going to solve all the country's problems," remarks ex-president Azali, who was also running for the presidency again, "their allegiance toward you grows rather quickly."

Sambi won his election in 2006, and, almost overnight, Kiwan became a fixture in Beit Salam, the presidential palace. "Bashar had carte blanche. He was Sambi's de facto prime minister," says Mohamed Sagaf, the former minister of foreign affairs. "Bashar's cook had more access to the president than members of parliament," remembers Houmed Msaidié, a close ally of President Azali's.

Kiwan and Sambi made a formidable team. Sambi would play the wise imam, forging alliances with fellow Muslims and raising the islands' profile through an increasing number of media appearances, in which he excelled. Kiwan would hustle on the Comorians' behalf abroad. He proved himself to be a natural, arranging talks between Sambi's cabinet and politicians and businessmen in the Gulf, who on several occasions came to the Comoros to hold bilateral negotiations. "Sambi's biggest flaw was that he didn't have the know-how to run a state," Kiwan recalls. "It was incredible [to me] that he received foreign delegations, but no one was even there to take minutes of the meetings." Sambi, in other words, required a manager, an adviser, an *eminence grise*, and Kiwan characterizes his role as a practical necessity. But he also had big ambitions for the Comoros.

His designs were in all likelihood bigger than the country's president could even conceive of: Kiwan says his inspiration in life is the Emirati ruler of Dubai. "Sheikh Mohammed bin

38   Rashid is a grand visionary, a man who completely transformed a country of 60,000 people, unknown as a travel destination," Kiwan tells me. "He didn't just change his country—he changed the global perception of the Arab citizen." The Comoros, at the dawn of the century, were Kiwan's Dubai. And it was a sign of the times—before the collapse of the global financial system, the revolutions in the Arab world, or before the real estate bubble burst—that it seemed not just possible, but probable, that the Comoros could be transformed into Hawaii for Arabs. "For me, it was a country where we could try something new, to build our success, to later show that we had participated in the launching of a nation," Kiwan says. "The dream was to become a pioneer in a country where there was everything left to build or re-build. That was what stimulated me."

In 2007, he was named honorary consul of Comoros to Kuwait—a post that came with a diplomatic passport to flash when jetting back and forth between the islands and the Middle East. And between meetings, he mapped out a Comorian business empire, drawing up elaborate plans for tourism, development, commerce, and trade, and pitching the projects to investors through a local company called Comoro Gulf Holding. According to Kiwan, CGH ended up raising around $100 million from his and Sheikh Sabah's friends and associates back home, though colleagues of Kiwan's at CGH say this sum has been vastly exaggerated. The senior CGH manager puts the number at closer to $10 to $15 million; he says all the money came from Kiwan, not from outside investors.

A country in as bad a shape as Comoros needs far more help than private investors can offer, though. In a meeting in

Sambi's office, Kiwan, accompanied by Sheikh Sabah, gave the
Comorians advice on how to develop their economy and finance
the large-scale projects he had for the islands. It was one thing
to solicit aid and look to the private sector for capital. But it
would be useful for the islands to give something in return—
a gesture, to show investors and Arab countries that they were
committed to interstate cooperation. The question was this:
What did Comoros have that other countries did not?

The answer was not ylang-ylang, or clove oil, or vanilla, the
main Comorian exports. It wasn't really tourism, either; beaches
are a dime a dozen for wealthy Arabs looking to travel.

What was needed was something only a small, remote state
like Comoros could provide, and that only a Gulf monarchy could
possibly demand.

The answer was passports—in bulk.

Market-Based Solution

The idea that a small country like Comoros could help an oil-rich economic behemoth solve a problem like statelessness is not an entirely original Kiwan enterprise. A similar deal was floated in 1997, under the presidency of Mohamed Taki Abdoulkarim, according to Mohamed Kalim Mze, a former secretary of state who now wears the distinctly louche title of "itinerant ambassador." Mze says he led talks discussing the possibility of a citizenship program with a Kuwaiti envoy in Johannesburg, and he claims they had detailed contracts drawn up. But President Taki died shortly thereafter, and the plan was left unexecuted.

Ultimately, it took a Kiwan to initiate a citizenship exchange of such epic proportions. If Denard was the ideal intermediary to provide offshore services for rogue regimes, Kiwan was the man for market-based solutions to global problems, delivered with an educated veneer of legitimacy—a Davos man, if you will. He understood, on a gut level, the geopolitical shifts that made the time ripe for such a transaction; his jet-set lifestyle, his work in media, and his enormous web of friends, business partners, and acquaintances no doubt contributed to this intuition.

As Kiwan tells it, he began to notice a growing demand for second passports among the Gulf's middle and upper classes. Having himself obtained his French nationality after living in Montpelier and marrying a Frenchwoman, he must have seen firsthand how much easier it was to travel and do business on a European passport than on his Syrian one. With his French papers and his impeccable accent, he was no longer Bashar, the sly Middle Eastern businessman with the shady Arab entourage. He was Mr. Kiwan, a father, husband, and respectable Montpelier media executive. A second nationality was a possibility not so much to *be* someone else, but to put a different foot forward when circumstances commanded it. It was a bit like having another face.

"People who live under repressive regimes are marginalized from the world, and live with the hope of obtaining a second nationality. The dream is to be American, Australian, Canadian," Kiwan told me. "But there are also countries like the Comoros whose passport offers few advantages but makes life easier for a lot of people." These countries, at the time, included a handful of Caribbean states that readily sold their citizenship to well-heeled foreigners, and virtually every major Western country that also offered fast-tracked citizenship via investor visas.

As Kiwan observed the wealthiest Middle Easterners collecting passports, he also grew aware of the plight of the *bidoon* across the Gulf, who had no passports, and the eagerness of the countries they lived in—notably, Kuwait and the United Arab

42   Emirates—to find a way to document their stateless population. Over the past decade, human rights organizations had
issued tersely worded recommendations for these countries to
resolve the problem, and some of the *bidoon* were even starting to demand political representation. But the regimes didn't
want to give the *bidoon* Kuwaiti or Emirati papers out of concern
that it would be expensive and politically fraught; they wanted a
more creative, market-based solution. If another country agreed
to naturalize the *bidoon*, everyone could be happy.

As an intermediary, Kiwan would win big, too. He found a
willing partner in the Emirati Interior Minister, Saif bin Zayed
Al Nahyan, and the director of his office, police chief Nasser
Salem Saif Lekhreiban Al Nuaimi, who seemed keen to strike a
deal and fast-forward the process. The Emirates had a history of
sending aid to the Comoros. Dubai World—a state-owned con-
glomerate that built "The World," an archipelago of 300 man-
made, still mostly undeveloped islands shaped like a world map
off the waterfront of Dubai—had announced plans to rehabili-
tate Galawa Beach, an old tourist resort run by South Africans
near where Bob Denard used to live. Amid the economic activity, Kiwan could do his work virtually unnoticed. Few had heard
of the Comoros anyway.

The Emiratis pledged to pay the Comoros $200 million in
state funds, or about one-quarter of the Comoros's annual GDP,
in exchange for the naturalization of some 4,000 *bidoon* families, according to statements later made by President Sambi.
According to a friend of Kiwan's in Kuwait City, he was handed
a check for $105 million by the Emiratis and told to go make
it happen.

Winning over the president was the easy part; Kiwan and his associates unwaveringly supported Sambi from the moment he took power, to the point where the government depended on him more than he depended on the government. During a fuel shortage, Kiwan's company, Comoro Gulf Holding, reportedly loaned the government three to five million dollars to keep the engines running. In early 2008, when a rogue colonel unsuccessfully tried to seize power on the Comorian island of Anjouan, Kiwan's company responded by printing and distributing posters of Sambi alongside the slogan "father of national unity."

Loyalty was only half the equation, though: Sambi desperately needed the money. A U.S. State Department cable noted that Sambi had inherited "an empty treasury and a substantial backlog of salary debt to teachers and civil servants." Taxi drivers had gone on strike for lack of decent roads, and hospital employees were walking off the job "because basic supplies, such as oxygen, are unavailable." "It was normal to accept [the citizenship deal]—it was the first time where we could help a fellow Muslim country," Sambi recalled in a speech. "I accepted knowing well that when dealing with such a rich country, the financial windfall would be obviously significant."

First, Kiwan and Sambi had to convince Parliament to turn the agreement into law.

"Bashar came back [from Kuwait] and insisted that this law had to pass for the Emiratis," the senior CGH manager told me. "I was just following directions. So we rounded up all the MPs who voted against the law, and we organized a trip to Kuwait."

44 After Kiwan picked the Comorians up at the airport, the men were shuttled away in limousines to a high-end hotel in Kuwait City to rest up. The next three days would be packed with meetings, dinners, sightseeing, and review sessions to go over the facts they had found and the lessons they had learned. The men had initially been promised a multi-leg journey through the Gulf—at least that's how they remember it—but previous plans to visit Qatar, Saudi Arabia, and the UAE were abruptly canceled "because the representatives with whom we were supposed to meet had gone to Europe to escape the heat," Sidi, the leader of the delegation, recalls being told.

It's not entirely clear why they were taken to Kuwait when it was the Emirates that had signed the initial deal for the passports; in any case, it didn't make much of a difference to the Comorians: a stateless person is stateless, regardless of the Gulf country they live in. And a Kuwait visit made sense for other reasons. Kiwan's connections in his home base certainly made it easy to impress his guests; it's a much freer society than the UAE, and it's possible that the Emiratis wanted to keep the deal under wraps and not make a show of carting their friends from the Indian Ocean around town.

Kiwan also appears to have had big ambitions for the Kuwaiti *bidoon*. The initial agreement he signed with the Comoros gave him the right to play the intermediary with all the Gulf countries, not just the UAE—meaning he could potentially mediate a deal to fix the nationalities of more than 100,000 people, and earn the commissions to match. Kiwan denies having had such intentions. But according to an old friend of his with whom he shared his plans on multiple occasions between 2007 and 2011, that was the

idea all along. Confidential feasibility studies commissioned by
Comoro Gulf Holding after the Emiratei deal was struck support
the claim, as do the recollections of the delegates, who say that
they specifically discussed documenting the Kuwaiti *bidoon*.

Kuwaiti representatives gave the Comorian delegation
promises of wealth, investment, and development. Kiwan made
a presentation on the tourism projects he had planned for the
Comoros, including a complete tourist village on the corniche
leading to the airport, complete with luxury amenities and a spa.

One evening, the men were invited to a lavish dinner hosted
by Sheikh Sabah, whose father, Jaber Al-Mubarak Al-Hamad
Al-Sabah, was then the Kuwaiti defense minister. After dinner,
Sabah gave the delegates laptops, watches, and, some say, enve-
lopes of cash. "Sabah didn't care about them—he made fun of
them," said a senior CGH manager who was present at the dinner.
As for the Comorians, "everyone had demands—they all wanted
different favors," recalls the guest.

But there was one more thing left to do: meeting the *bidoon*.
The Comorians had never met one of their future compatriots.
Who were these people without a nation? How could one be at
once native and without a land? In a hotel conference room, the
delegates spoke to several stateless men and women. "I don't
know where he found these *bidoon*. It could well have been
Kiwan's driver, for all I knew. But it didn't matter at all to the
Comorians. All they wanted to do was sleep, eat, have fun, and
shop," said the senior manager. Through an interpreter, they
gave a full account of their situation: why they were stateless, what they did, how much money they had, and how the
Comoro Islands could help them.

46   Mohamed Sagaf, who was used to taking trips to negotiate investments as minister of foreign affairs, was puzzled by
this crash course in statelessness. "Each country has its par-
ticularities, but this was really something," Sagaf told me.
"They explained to us that the bidoon were people of the desert, nomads. They said they hadn't wanted to settle in cities
because their way of life was the desert, camels, sheep . . . so
when the elders refused [to take citizenship], the children
ended up victims."

But Sagaf was baffled that Kuwait didn't want to grant citizenship to such a large population of its native-born residents,
and his colleagues could not grasp why the bidoon would want to
be citizens of the Comoros at all.

Particularly strange was when two members of the same
family reportedly explained that one of them was bidoon, while
the other had Kuwaiti nationality. This can happen when citizenship is granted through marriage, or when one ancestor
registered but another did not. The Comorians withheld their
ambivalence out of courtesy. "We can't judge a foreign country,
particularly an Arab country," Sagaf said. "You can't tell them
they're doing the wrong thing and that they should rectify it."

The men were often misled, or simply missed the point—
it's unclear which. "It turned out they were citizens of nowhere
because they were nomads living in the desert," Ibrahim
M'houmadi Sidi told me. "Some of the bidoon had become rich
and wanted to travel and send their kids abroad—activities you
need a passport for." This is inaccurate. While there are wealthy
and well-connected bidoon families, most are poor relative
to the citizen population. Very few bidoon lead nomadic lives

anymore. The men were also apparently told that the *bidoon* who were to receive Comorian passports under the given plan would personally invest in the islands, and eventually receive nationality of the country where they lived. "They were only to hold the Comorian passport temporarily," Sidi says. "That way, they could register their presence and after some time, collect their nationality."

The deal, in other words, was pitched as a stopgap measure for the benefit of wealthy investors who just so happened to be stateless. That's a much more attractive prospect than having to take in a large group of strangers from another country. Out of ignorance, willful or genuine, the Comorians played along. Every evening, Sidi would gather the men in his hotel room to go over what they'd learned that day. "The whole delegation unanimously agreed on the fact that the project was important and that it could help us reinforce our relations with the country," he recalls.

There, their ideas about an "economic citizenship" program took shape. They did not want to blatantly allow for the naturalization of the *bidoon*, but they were perfectly happy to grant outsiders "economic" citizenship—which did not include the right to vote in local elections, nor reside in the Comoros permanently—in exchange for "investments" in their country. This applied whether the applicants were stateless or had six passports, whether they intended to visit the Comoros or not. Thirty countries had done this already, they recall Kiwan telling them. This is partially true—dozens of countries, including the U.S. and Canada, grant residence and work permits, but not full citizenship, in exchange for capital investments.

48   After three days in Kuwait, and satisfied with the information they had gathered, the Comorians packed their bags full of
gifts and headed back to the private plane to return home. But
there was one more surprise left. On the way to the Comoros,
their jet stopped in Dubai, where the men were taken to the Burj
Al Arab, the famous sail-shaped seven-star hotel. It's the fourth
tallest hotel building in the world, and a large suite on a high floor
had been rented out for them. The men were impressed—there
are no elevators in the Comoros—and they spent the afternoon
lounging, relaxing, and shopping, all on Bashar's dime.

Six weeks later, the men gathered in the National Assembly to
debate and vote on the economic citizenship bill. The text spoke
simply of granting papers to "partners" of the Comoro Islands
from all countries, so long as these partners did not have criminal records, belong to terrorist organizations, or threaten the
social and cultural cohesion of the country. New citizens "naturalized" under this procedure would obtain passports but not
the right to vote, serve in the armed forces, or run for office; it
was a kind of hack by which the country would recognize these
citizens as their own on paper, but grant them very few privileges in person. "Basically, the person doesn't have Comorian
citizenship," Sidi explains. "His only right is to have a passport,
invest in the Comoros, and if there's a problem, address it with the
local tribunal."

      Because the bill had become the talk of the town, the debate
was broadcast on the radio. The discussion grew so heated that
the president of the parliament, Dhoifir Bounou, stormed out in
frustration. He was soon joined by fifteen others, most of them

members of the opposition party. But Sidi, the parliament's vice
president and the most prominent opposition figure, stayed
behind. By then the lights had been turned off, so the remaining
deputies proceeded by candlelight. Acting against his party's
wishes and armed with four proxy votes, Sidi, along with thir-
teen remaining delegates, voted unanimously in favor of the
proposal. One week later, amidst continuing public discontent,
the bill was signed into law by President Sambi.

The Reluctant Cosmopolite

Ahmad Abdul Khaleq, a vocal blogger who had become one of the fiercest activists for the rights of stateless people, knew nothing about the Comoro Islands when he became a citizen of the tiny country on May 21, 2012. An official in Abu Dhabi handed him a passport—something he'd wanted all his life. But unfortunately, the country that had issued it was not the United Arab Emirates, where Khaleq was born and had lived his entire life; nor Balochistan, the once-independent Pakistani province from which his ancestors had emigrated generations ago. Before this day, he himself was stateless, or *bidoon*, like up to 100,000 people in the Emirates, and up to 15 million in the world. Suddenly, the nation to which he belonged was a small archipelago in the Indian Ocean.

"All I knew about the Comoros was from books about the old Arab explorers," Khaleq says. "I never expected that one day I would be a citizen of this country." Khaleq, who is stocky and short, with a broad brow, a square face, and a deep dimple that forks a stubbly chin, leafed through his new passport with a mixture of frustration and curiosity. After a baffling series of events, he was no longer a legal fiction in the eyes of the government.

Most people take their citizenships for granted; Khaleq didn't have one. Born in the emirate of Sharjah on May 5, 1977, and raised there and in nearby Ajman, Khaleq hadn't noticed being treated any differently from anyone around him. He lived with his mother, father, and six sisters in a big two-story house with six rooms and a yard. He was a good student and a hard worker. He drank tea on the beach with his friends, caught fish in the sea, and warmed his hands by small outdoor fires on chilly desert nights. Things were easy then, he remembers. Everyone knew each other.

Growing up, Khaleq didn't feel stateless; he felt local. He knew no other community. Both sides of his family emigrated in the 1940s and '50s, he says, when unrest in their native Balochistan drove them to flee the region. So their presence in the country predates the existence of the United Arab Emirates, which was only formed in 1971, after its six semi-autonomous emirates of Abu Dhabi, Ajman, Dubai, Fujairah, Sharjah, and Umm al-Quwain declared independence from the British. (A seventh, Ras al-Khaimah, joined the federation in 1972. Bahrain and Qatar were invited to join the union, but they declined.) Previously, each emirate had been overseen by an individual ruling family, so there wasn't a strong, pre-existing sense of unifying Emirati nationalism among its people, or a bill of rights and an emotionally charged set of

52   patriotic duties and obligations. The Arabian Peninsula was for centuries largely inhabited by nomadic tribes and traveling merchants, so it was a little absurd from the outset to claim that anyone was more "native" to a given patch of desert than anyone else. Put another way, everyone was *bidoon* until someone decided they weren't.

"In Emirati society, ordinary people did not make a differentiation between themselves," Khaleq says. When he speaks about his predicament, he alternates between sounding like the consummate activist—confident, determined, angry, gesticulating dramatically, and accusing the authorities of his former home of grave abuses—and an orphaned child who wants nothing more than a home.

"People generally know that the *bidoon*'s situation is not their own fault. People cannot say, 'Well, you are *bidoon* because you are Balochi,' because they themselves are often from elsewhere—Saudi Arabia, or Oman," he goes on. "It is a problem created by the state." (Some *bidoon* are, or were, part of the Bedouin tribe; others are not. The two words are often confused but mean different things.)

Noora Lori, an assistant professor of international relations at Boston University who studies migrants in the Gulf, says that when Khaleq was born, the administrative structures that ultimately led to the government making distinctions between natives and foreigners didn't exist. "In the UAE, [discrimination] depends more on which emirate you come from," Lori says. "But within that, key families got narrated into what Emiratis should be, and certain others were not seen as too viable. Minorities and people from smaller emirates end up

being less incorporated." (The motivations for discrimination   53
varied by country; in Kuwait, some of the discrimination was
based on tribal affiliation.)

What's more, the concept of nationality in the region was
an unfamiliar one when these states were formed, and many
people who are now stateless fell through the cracks: they
didn't, couldn't, or weren't called upon to register. Many
didn't see the point of obtaining a passport. Some of them
were nomadic, and some of them simply traveled often. In that
part of the world, this wasn't unusual.

Khaleq's father, a civil servant who had always lived within
modern-day Emirate borders, had failed to obtain and renew
the necessary paperwork to formally become a citizen after the
country was founded. The concept of registering as a national
was new to the senior Khaleq. He lived in the Emirates, had been
born in the Emirates, and even worked at the Ministry of the
Interior, Ahmed says. He didn't feel that he needed papers to
prove anything.

It was a grave mistake, and he wasn't alone in making it. As
the Emirates gradually became a more powerful nation-state,
it contended that those without papers were not native to the
land, and therefore had no place in the oil-rich society. As time
passed, it became more and more important to provide formal
proof of citizenship to receive any kind of government services. Having missed their window, nothing has come of the
Khaleqs' dozens of claims to citizenship. Without a passport,
Khaleq hadn't been allowed to cross borders, so he had never
left the Emirates. For the *bidoon*, even a pilgrimage to Mecca
requires special permission. (The 15-year-old Khaleq got the

54 chance to go to Mecca on a scholarship, but he turned down the opportunity in a fit of of teenage rebellion, he says.)

Claire Beaugrand, a scholar who studies migration in the Gulf states at the French Institute for the Near East, traces the region's statelessness problem to the traditions of the region and the end of colonialism. After the Gulf states achieved independence, "the regime of free movements, comings and goings across the Persian Gulf or the North-Arabian desert [were] replaced by a system of regulated migrations where modern states use legal tools of control, such as nationality, visas and residency permits," Beaugrand wrote in a paper, "Nationality and Migration Controls in the Gulf Countries." As the Emirates and their neighbors became active participants in a world characterized by United Nations Security Council votes, population surveys, and oil-fueled development, they took on the trappings of a European-style nation-state. They created structures that distinguished between natives, foreigners, guest workers, and illegals, even if it didn't make sense to suddenly transpose these categories on a historically tribal, nomadic population and land with fresh borders.

The result was that national identification "came to replace the existing form of traditional identification that is membership of a tribe, place of origin, or professional activity," according to Beaugrand. "The population that found themselves in an in-between situation [became] victims of their having no territorial anchor."

Even those who were grounded, like Khaleq's father, saw little point in anchoring themselves, if only with a piece of paper.

A stateless population was born, and the government did little to help it.

In *The Origins of Totalitarianism*, the philosopher Hannah Arendt, who was stateless for more than a decade during and after the Second World War, famously described citizenship as "the right to have rights." What do human rights even mean, Arendt probed, if they depend so largely on the assignment of a citizenship by a particular country, rather than a common shared humanity? Being arbitrarily denied nationality is a kind of first-order deprivation that carries over into all parts of life. Unlike food or shelter, citizenship cannot simply be conferred to those who most need it by well-meaning individuals, a charitable organization, or the United Nations—which, in November 2014, launched a ten-year initiative to end the problem of statelessness around the world. The campaign depends not on enforceable law, but on public pressure. It is entirely up to a sovereign nation whom it does or does not accept as one of its own, and there's little anyone else can do about it.

Fixing statelessness isn't technically very difficult; it can be solved with some basic organization and paperwork. But the political will to help and even acknowledge the problem is what's often lacking. The Emirati government, for instance, contends that there are fewer than 5,000 *bidoon* living within its territorial borders; it has said in the past that many residents who claim to be stateless are covering up their real nationality in order to stay in the Emirates. But Refugees International, an advocacy group, puts the number closer to 100,000. There

56   is also a sizable *bidoon* population in Kuwait, Qatar, and Saudi
     Arabia, where, in 2013, a stateless man doused himself in gaso-
     line and set himself on fire in public. Accurate statistics are
     hard to come by. "It's a very politicized issue, and highly secre-
     tive in terms of what gets released," Noora Lori says. The UN
     estimates that there are just shy of 100,000 stateless people
     in Kuwait and 70,000 in Saudi Arabia. And the governments,
     despite claiming to want to resolve this situation, have barely
     done so.

     Statelessness in the twenty-first century is confounding
     for another reason: globalization. In a world governed by free
     trade, the fate of the stateless is largely dependent on whether
     the nation in which they were born will accept them. Edward
     Kleinbard, a tax law professor at the University of Southern
     California, has been studying the topic of stateless income:
     money generated by multinational companies which, thanks to
     loopholes and creative accounting, has no discernible country
     of origin. "Stateless persons wander a hostile globe, looking
     for asylum," Kleinbard noted in a paper. "By contrast, stateless
     income takes a bearing for any of a number of zero or low-tax
     jurisdictions, where it finds a ready welcome."

     Such are the paradoxical effects of globalization. While
     corporate entities are able to take full advantage of the oppor-
     tunities presented to them—cheap foreign labor, lower taxes,
     bigger markets—the people these companies depend on to
     buy, sell, and create their products are still forcibly contained
     and constrained by the territories that claim them, if they're
     lucky enough to have one at all.

As Diogenes and Zeno pointed out a long time ago, all borders are constructs. The lines in the sand between Saudi Arabia and the Emirates are no more meaningful than the ones separating the United States and Mexico. In *Imagined Communities,* Benedict Anderson explains that it takes time for free-floating ideas surrounding nationhood and nationality, or "imagining," to boil down to a cohesive glue, and for borders to carry any real meaning.

"In the modern conception, state sovereignty is fully, flatly, and evenly operative over each square centimeter of legally demarcated territory," Anderson writes. "But in the older imagining . . . borders were porous and indistinct, and sovereignties faded imperceptibly into one another." The newer the country, the fresher the boundaries, and the more arbitrary the distinctions between those who are said to belong inside and those who belong outside.

These distinctions and exclusions can serve a political purpose. As the Emirates gained global economic prominence, statelessness was left unresolved in part because of the country's wealth. The richer the state got exporting oil, the more people rushed there seeking employment, and the more defensive the ruling elite grew about establishing themselves as the only beneficiaries of this bounty. In the UAE, the population ballooned from about a million residents in 1980 to 9 million today, but the added bodies were disproportionately foreign ones. Emirati citizens currently make up around 15 percent of the population, and male Emirati citizens receive benefits that would make a Scandinavian social democracy blush: an annual, no-strings-

58 attached stipend of around $55,000 per year; free land on which to build a house; a no-interest loan to finance it; a marriage bonus of almost $20,000; subsidized utilities; and the free healthcare and education that all Emiratis receive as a matter of course, and that many *bidoon* are denied or have trouble registering for.

The story of the *bidoon* in neighboring countries follows a similar arc. While the "native" elites established themselves as rulers, grew rich, and lived off their state's profligacy, an army of *bidoon*, expatriates, and guest workers failed to secure long-term residence permits, citizenship, or any real rights. Their sheer numbers pushed the countries' rulers to think deeply about national identity and draw up policies separating "us" from "them."

"The differing sub-communities . . . are not being equally 'imagined,'" notes Neil Patrick, a researcher who taught political science at the American University of Sharjah, alluding to Anderson's theory. "Existential fears are deepening the state-building efforts of largely new nations whose leaders are 'inventing' the national community."

Kuwait, for instance, treated the *bidoon* as citizens until the late eighties, but in 1985 declared they were now foreigners living in Kuwait illegally. The reasons for this reclassification ranged from tribal and religious discrimination to electoral politics and shrinking government coffers. According to a 2009 U.S. diplomatic cable, the sharp drop in oil prices in 1984 and 1985 likely caused Kuwait to be concerned about the number of people who could receive government benefits. Granting the *bidoon* full citizenship could also have skewed elections in Kuwait to the benefit of ascendant rural and tribal members of parliament at the expense of the urban elite. In its 1988 state surveys, the government subtracted the *bidoon* population from its count of citizens and added them to the foreign resident category. By 1990, the *bidoon* "were living in abject poverty, having been dismissed in large numbers from their jobs in the civilian government and private sector," according to a 1995 Human Rights Watch report. "They were also living under the threat of deportation."

It was the First Gulf War that truly brought tensions to the surface. On August 2, 1990, Saddam Hussein's Iraqi Army invaded Kuwait, driving away the royal family and killing the Emir's youngest brother. It was not a long war—by late February, U.S.-backed coalition forces were able to free the country—but it was a deeply traumatic incident for the Kuwaitis. Nearly 2,000 Kuwaitis were killed by Iraqi forces, and over 600, likely over 700 of the country's 2,011 (1,330 active) oil wells were burned and destroyed.

In the months during and after the war, Kuwait began to view the *bidoon* with increasing suspicion, and accused many of defecting to the other side. The basis for this claim was an order by the occupying authorities informing all noncitizen Kuwaiti residents that they must join a pro-Saddam militia called the Popular Army that would support the Iraqi forces, or face imprisonment and death. It's unclear how many *bidoons* served or even registered, but what is clear is that by the Kuwaiti government's own 1995 estimate, 25 percent of Kuwait's army of 20,000 were *bidoon*, and before the Iraq war, the number was closer to 80 percent. It's estimated that one-third of fatalities on the Kuwaiti side were *bidoon*. "Seizing

60   on the fact that a few individual Bedoons joined the Popular
Army, many Kuwaits have indicted all Bedoons for collaboration,"
Human Rights Watch noted. "In their hunt for collaborators,
Kuwaiti authorities and individuals have overlooked the fact
that Bedoons fought valiantly against the Iraqi invasion."

After it was liberated from the Iraqi army, Kuwait ramped
up its discrimination against the *bidoon*. It began withholding
basic services from these residents while putting pressure on
them to reveal their "true" nationality, a practice that persists.
Noora Lori notes that the war had an effect across the Gulf states
analogous to the attacks of September 11, 2001 in the United
States. Security became an enormous concern, and there was a
parallel movement to draw distinctions between people, in part
to build a sense of national identity within the new state. "You
had this idea that you really need to have everyone in a category,
and have documentation for everybody," she says.

Kuwait's policies sent a ripple throughout the Gulf countries. The neighboring states began drawing starker distinctions between "natives" and "outsiders," making it difficult for
anyone, *bidoon* or not, to naturalize as a citizen. Khaleq's *bidoon*
community in Ajman had to pay for education, while Emiratis
went to school for free. Then it became harder for them to obtain
birth certificates and death certificates, and to keep certain jobs.

In the early 2000s, Kuwaiti *bidoon* began to point out the
unfairness of these actions in Internet forums, and Ahmed
Abdul Khaleq found a common cause. "I saw what the Kuwaiti
bidoon were writing: 'We have no rights, no health card, no
driver license,'" he recalls. "And inside my mind I started to
build my ideas and writing myself: 'We are *bidoon*, we have

rights, we are born here, our father was born here and grandfather was born here. Others in our position have nationality.
Why don't we?'"

At the time, Khaleq was working in the back office of the
police department in Ajman. He made a relatively good living,
but the rift between Emiratis and their stateless counterparts
was widening. As Dubai erected a glittering metropolis from the
sand, Khaleq remembers thinking that he couldn't even get a
library card.

The Emirati authorities, too, wanted the *bidoon* problem to
go away. By 2006, Sheikh Khalifa bin Zayed Al Nahyan, president of the UAE, promised to figure out a way to document the
bidoon. His first move was to allow Emirati women to pass down
citizenship to their children—previously, citizenship could
only be passed on through patrilineal lines. The government
then announced it had opened up the naturalization process
so that the *bidoon* could apply to be documented, but the government has since released very little data on naturalization.
In March 2008, Bloomberg News reported that just 1,294 of
100,000 Emirati *bidoon* had received Emirati citizenship since
Sheikh Khalifa's 2006 pledge, partly because applications were
being handled on a strict case-by-case basis. It also established
an agency to register residents who didn't have papers. This
agency reportedly pressured *bidoon* to reveal any other passports they might have or be entitled to. "Many *bidoon* have come
forward and revealed their country of origin," a spokesman for
the Ministry of Interior told Reuters in 2008. "As a result, the
UAE government has waived all penalties for having resided in
the UAE illegally."

62   These initiatives certainly didn't help Khaleq, who, like many, had no other papers to speak of, nor any country to claim as his own. Frustrated, in 2009 he began posting on a website called UAE Hewar, or the Emirati Dialogue. It was founded by Ahmed Mansoor, an engineer, outspoken pro-democracy activist, and member of Human Rights Watch who also blogged on the site. Despite being born Emirati, Mansoor has been accused of being a "traitor without a nation" for his dissident activities. The site was a place where Emiratis could discuss politics and culture. "It was the only forum that allowed people to talk freely online, and it attracted lots of people who had things to say," Mansoor says. "Ahmed was one of them."

In the forums, Khaleq used a pseudonym—Emirati Bidoon. "He was not really well-known then," Mansoor recalls. But taking a cue from his stateless Kuwaiti compadres, Khaleq demanded rights for the *bidoon* in fiery posts, and also supported initiatives for the devolution of some power from the sheikhs to the people. The seven emirates are currently each governed by an emir, who has absolute power. The emir of Abu Dhabi, Sheikh Khalifa bin Zayed Al Nahyan, who succeeded his father as the second president of the UAE, appoints half of a forty-member advisory body called the Federal National Council, while the other twenty are elected by a regionally selected electoral committee.

In December 2010, protests in Tunisia sparked what became known as the Arab Spring. The rulers of Tunisia, Egypt, Libya, and Yemen were ousted; civil war erupted in Syria; uprisings began in Bahrain; and protests broke out in Algeria, Jordan, Morocco, Saudi Arabia, Oman, and many other Arab nations.

The unrest didn't come close to inciting a Tahrir Square-style revolution in the Gulf states, but it sent rumblings of discontent and rattled the ruling elites there.

Kuwait's version of the Arab Spring is believed to have been initiated by the *bidoon* and their supporters, who took to the streets to demand more rights in February and March 2011. They had no plans to overthrow the government; on the contrary, they appeared "waving the country's flag and clutching pictures of the Emir," the BBC reported. They did, however, demand citizenship and the rights that come with it. Police used tear gas and water cannon to disperse the crowd. Other protesters stormed the National Assembly and boycotted elections; prime minister Nasser Mohammed Al-Ahmed Al-Sabah and his cabinet resigned while the parliament was dissolved.

Authorities across the Gulf reacted swiftly to contain and crush what little dissent made its way inside their borders. They used a carrot-and-stick approach, dispensing cash bonuses (to citizens, naturally) and investing in infrastructure and services to quell unease, all while arresting activists and dissidents to set an example.

Since life was good for Emirati citizens and precarious for everyone else under the authoritarian regime, there wasn't much opportunity for revolt there, but the group that came to be known as the "UAE Five"—with Khaleq as a member of the quintet—was an exception.

Trouble for the Five began in March 2011, when more than a hundred people signed an online petition calling for universal participation in electing the Federal National Council and for giving the body legislative powers. A few weeks later, Nasser bin Ghaith, an economics lecturer at the Abu Dhabi branch of the Paris-Sorbonne University, published a paper analyzing the effects of the nascent Arab Spring in the UAE.

On April 8, police officers arrived at Khaleq's house in the early morning. "Fifteen people, four cars, just for me," Khaleq recalls. "I thought, am I Osama Bin Laden?" Three days later, police arrested Mansoor. Bin Ghaith and two bloggers, Fahad Salim Dalk and Hassan Ali al-Khamis, were also arrested.

The UAE Five were charged two months later with publicly insulting the country's rulers, which is a crime under Emirati penal code, and with disrupting public order for statements they had made. UAE Hewar was shut down by the authorities in 2010.

Amnesty International immediately called for their release and launched a large-scale advocacy campaign that made its way as far as the stage of the Edinburgh festival. Several prominent academics, including the moral philosopher Thomas Nagel and legal scholar Ronald Dworkin, signed an open letter in the *New York Review of Books* expressing their concern. The BBC and the *New York Times* covered the arrests, but local independent media were prohibited from doing so. Government-controlled outlets called them religious extremists and agents for Iran.

Khaleq only met his alleged co-conspirators in jail, and he shared a cell with Mansoor for a couple of weeks. Mansoor is a well-known and respected activist in the Emirates, and Khaleq had hoped to make his acquaintance, but not under those circumstances. "I said, 'I'm broken,'" Khaleq recalls. "And he said, 'No, you have to keep going. Even in the dark place there is hope.'"

Khaleq was the only one among the five who was stateless. A closed-door trial began in June in Abu Dhabi, which Human Rights Watch denounced as "having no legitimate legal or factual basis." In October, the prisoners boycotted the trial, and they staged a twenty-day hunger strike the next month. A panel of four judges sentenced Mansoor to three years in prison; Khaleq and the remaining detainees received two-year jail sentences, and Khaleq, who was ordinarily on the roly-poly side, stopped the hunger strike. "We tried to strike to pressure the government and the court to let us go home, but I got two years, and Ahmed Mansoor got three years," he says. "I told him, 'We failed. I'll stop the hunger strike.' And he said, 'it's up to you.'"

One day later, Sheikh Khalifa issued a presidential pardon for the five. He did not give a reason. Khaleq and his companions were released. "I feel happy because I am back with my family," bin Ghaith told the Associated Press. "But I also feel ashamed and have deep sorrow for my country. All I can say is that it's a sad moment for our homeland, a beginning of a police state that has tarnished the image of the UAE forever."

Undeterred by his detention, Khaleq started writing again, with renewed enthusiasm. He started his own blog, Emirati Bidoon. "After [my arrest] I wanted to challenge the government," Khaleq recalls. "And we got famous! Ahmed Mansoor got famous, I got more famous, so every one of us had a case. Ahmed Mansoor was asking for more democracy; I had a case for stateless people. And I said, 'We want our rights. Why are we still stateless?'"

According to Khaleq, the government tried to pay them to keep quiet. "We met the ruler of Ras al Khaimah, and he [said],

'Please don't speak, don't do anything, you'll get everything you want but keep quiet. Go to Abu Dhabi and the people will give you everything, just keep quiet,'"he says. "The five of us, we sat together and decided not to go to Abu Dhabi, not to take any money, and that was it."

It was during this period that Khaleq became Comorian. There was no oath or ceremony; he didn't even ask for it. His "natural-ization" began with a phone call from a man who asked to speak to his father and said that he had orders from the government to tell the family to come in and apply for Comorian passports. "He said that if we applied for citizenship, we would without a doubt later receive Emirati citizenship," Khaleq recalls.

The scheme, scholars and activists say, was publicized through statements by government officials that held up one resourceful *bidoon* named Abdul Rahman as an example. The man was said to have obtained Comorian papers, and then used them to apply for Emirati citizenship. Interior Minister Saif bin Zaid Al Nahyan said he was impressed by Rahman's personal initiative, and issued a recommendation that his Comorian papers be replaced with Emirati ones. "The fact that he sought to correct his status to stay and work legally in the country proves that he is well-intentioned," he told journalists

But the notion that the *bidoon* had much of a choice in the Comoros matter was also an illusion.

"The government prevented us from doing anything: reg-istering our children's births, renewing your driver's license, renewing your health insurance card—marrying, even," Khaleq says. "So the Comoros passport became the only solution."

When Khaleq went to renew his license plates, he was turned away. "They told me that they had directives from the Interior Ministry not to, unless and until I applied for Comoros citizenship," he says. "It got to the point where they told me, 'If you don't apply for Comoros citizenship, Ahmed, we will not perform any services for you.'"

Finally, Khaleq and his father went to apply at a two-story building with a Comorian flag flying outside. The office wasn't staffed by Africans, Khaleq recalls, but by locals speaking perfect Arabic. Some of them were *bidoon* who had received Comorian passports themselves, according to a Comorian official who visited the office. They returned two or three more times to the office over the following weeks with Khaleq's six sisters and his mother. The family received their passports a few weeks later—only to be told that they must apply for residence visas to remain in the Emirates legally.

"They rang from the passport office and told my father to come and bring his whole family with him to sign some papers," Khaleq remembers. "It was just me, my father, and my mother in the house that day. So we went to the passport authority, and when we arrived I was told they wanted to speak to me alone outside the office. Everyone felt that it all was a bit strange." He was then led outside to the back of the building and toward a white car with tinted windows. There were two policemen sitting inside the car. They opened the door and told him to get in.

The first jail they took Khaleq to was in the Wathba district of Abu Dhabi. The prison prides itself on its clean, modern interior and its humane treatment of inmates. "We live in a globalized

68   world and most of our prisoners are deported after their sen-
      tences," the warden of Wathba told the *Abu Dhabi National*
      newspaper in 2014. "If they had been abused at our correctional
      facilities in any way then they would speak about it when they
      went home."

      Next, Khaleq was sent to another jail in Al Shahamah, a quiet
      neighborhood on the outskirts of Abu Dhabi and a 30-minute
      drive away from the passport authority. Around 300 people of
      different nationalities sat crammed in ten small holding cells,
      as Khaleq remembers it. Unnamed guards spat insults. He was a
      dissident, they said. He did not belong in the UAE.

      Technically, they were right. He spent about a week in Al
      Shahamah before being transferred to yet another jail, where
      a Palestinian prison mate told Khaleq that he'd been in jail
      for thirteen years for a drug offense. "May God help you. Lord
      knows how long you will stay here," he told Khaleq.

      Khaleq was put in solitary confinement. "We were in com-
      plete isolation," he says. "In solitary you become mad. I need to
      speak with somebody! Like, 'Hey, how are you? I am bored, you
      are bored like me!'" It was hard not talking. Khaleq is a chatty
      man, ready to share his opinions on matters serious and trivial.
      He speaks English well and astonishingly fast, and he talks in
      his native Arabic even faster. But when he was transferred to
      another cell, it was full of Bangladeshis and Indians. They didn't
      speak Arabic, and Khaleq doesn't speak Hindi. Khaleq began to
      fight with the guards, refusing to answer commands or to eat. It
      worked—they took him to a block shared with Arabs. Little did
      he know that he would have to get used to living in countries full
      of people who don't speak his language.

When he was a *bidoon*, Khaleq couldn't be deported. Countries typically refuse entry to visitors who have no home which they can return to. But he was now a Comorian citizen. His interlocutors were devising just the plan.

"They would say, 'Okay, Ahmed! What do you say we send you to Afghanistan, to Iran, or to Pakistan?'" he recalls. The Comoro Islands were conspicuously absent from his list of options. That's because the Comorians had issued his passport with the stipulation that they didn't want him around. Khaleq had no interest in this so-called homeland. After he turned down Afghanistan, Iran, and Pakistan, he was given a chance to go to Thailand. He reluctantly agreed. He would get his freedom, but he could never go home.

The warden called Khaleq's father and told him to take the Comorian passport to the Thai embassy and obtain a two-month visitor visa, then buy him a plane ticket to Bangkok. Khaleq's father delivered the immigration papers to the prison with a two-way ticket attached, even though it was made clear to him that his son would only be making a one-way trip.

Khaleq was escorted straight from prison to the airport by a police officer who recognized him as a classmate from a commuter college. "He said, 'How did you come to this situation?'" Khaleq recalls. "And I said, 'This is life. If someone speaks up for his rights, he has to be in this situation.'" He walked out of the car and through the terminal, overcome with emotion. His family was not allowed to be there to say farewell, so he simply boarded the plane with no luggage, still wearing his prison clothes. After many years of fighting for his rights, Khaleq had gotten his wish—he was no longer stateless.

The Man Who Sold the World

"Sometimes it is necessary to dissemble one's nationality."
—Evelyn Waugh, *Scoop*

On a humid afternoon in September 2014, Christian Kalin held court before a crowd of lawyers, bankers, and accountants in a conference room at the Four Seasons hotel in midtown Manhattan. He was there to talk about his lifelong passion: passports.

Kalin, a slight, stiff-limbed man, held up a red rectangle embossed with tidy crosses for the crowd to see. "If there's something I've learned in my life, it's that having more than one passport is very useful," he said, pacing back and forth across the room, his thick eyebrows brooding, his posture angled slightly forward.

Kalin, however, is a citizen of Switzerland—and according

to *The Economist*, the landlocked confederation is the best country on the planet in which to be born. And for good reason: The Swiss passport gives its owner the right to travel visa-free to 170 countries out of a possible 196; to live in peaceful, clean, well-financed, well-governed villages, towns, and cities; to participate in one of the most functional direct democracies in the world; and to hold secret bank accounts (at least for now). Of the world's eight billion people, only about seven million are lucky enough to be Swiss—a remarkable privilege that Ayelet Shachar, a citizenship scholar at the University of Toronto, likens to winning the "birthright lottery."

"You might wonder: why does a Swiss guy who has a Swiss passport need another one?" Kalin asked.

There's a motto in the citizenship industry: You can never be too rich, be too thin, or have too many passports.

Kalin, who has at least five passports, is the chairman of Henley & Partners, a private consulting firm that helps the wealthy buy citizenships and residence permits, and advises countries on how to sell them. The citizenship-by-investment programs that Kalin hawks are different from the Comorian arrangement. His mostly Caribbean and European client states usually require applicants to pass extensive tests and fill out a lot of forms. The passports aren't sold in bulk to another government, but to privileged individuals spending a lot of money; they're supplementing their portfolio of passports, not starting their collection. These "global citizens" are anything but stateless on paper; but in spirit, they see little need to confine themselves to a fixed home.

Kalin has emerged as the go-to guy in this industry. No

one knows passports or believes so deeply in holding additional citizenships as Chris Kalin. Nor has anyone been so instrumental in presenting citizenship as a commodity that can be bought and sold, or has so single-mindedly thought about the economic, political, and moral implications thereof, as Christian Kalin.

Kalin has worked with the nations of Malta, St. Kitts and Nevis, and Antigua and Barbuda. Henley & Partners also caters to individuals, including Bashar Kiwan's cohort in the Middle East and their contemporaries in Russia, China, India, and beyond. These people are referred to with an unwieldy acronym: UHNWIs, or ultra-high net worth individuals. The UHNWIs often arrive at Henley's doorsteps via their financial advisers, who over the past decade or so have added citizenship and residence planning to their laundry list of wealth management and preservation strategies. The language that they use is telling. It's not about buying passports; it's about self-actualizing as a global citizen.

"Today, a person of talent and means need not limit his or her life and business to only one country," reads a Henley brochure. "Making an active decision with regard to your residence and citizenship gives you more personal freedom, privacy, and security."

For those in the market for a second (or third) passport, the range of options has never been more plentiful. It is possible, as of this writing, to become, through completely legal and legitimate means, a citizen of St. Kitts and Nevis, Antigua and Barbuda, Grenada, the Commonwealth of Dominica, Malta, Bulgaria, Cyprus, and Austria. The documents can be bought for $200,000 (Dominica) or millions of Euros (Austria, Malta). Since the 2008 financial crisis, a new country has been added to the list almost every year. Henley imitators are cropping up in Shanghai, Singapore, and Dubai.

Freedom to travel is a major reason why someone would spend a couple hundred thousand dollars on citizenship. For all the talk of an interconnected, "flat" world, being born with a bad passport is still a great misfortune. People with "good" passports don't think about them much. But people with "bad" passports think of them a great deal. To the wealthy, this is particularly insulting: A bad passport is like a phantom limb that won't stop tingling no matter how much money, power, or success they've accumulated—a constant reminder that the playing field is never truly level, and that life for your average Canadian billionaire will be easier than for a billionaire from Botswana or Peru.

Henley's pitch to these people is this: In the modern world, borders are still very much erect—but they can be flattened, for a price. To drive the point home, Henley creates a yearly ranking, published by *The Economist*, showing which passports are the worst and the best. Finland, Germany, Sweden, and the United Kingdom tie for first place; Afghanistan comes in 94th, with visa-free access to just 28 nations.

But there are more reasons why, for the modern UHNWI, being just Indonesian or French is no longer enough. An extra passport can help diversify their investments and reduce their tax bill. It can allow them to conduct business more easily in other countries and lower the barriers to educating their children abroad. It can serve as a safety net; for decades, wary

74   oligarchs from the former Soviet Union have flocked to London, Cyprus, and Geneva to establish residence. In certain countries a second passport or residence has become practically *de rigueur*. In 2011, Henley's CEO told me they'd seen a surge in interest from the Middle East in the months after the Arab Spring. And in 2014, Ihor Kolomoisky, the right-wing banker-turned governor of Dniepropitrovsk, in Ukraine, was asked in an interview about his Ukrainian, Israeli, and Cypriot citizenships. The journalist pointed out that dual nationality is prohibited by the Ukrainian constitution. "Yes," Kolomoisky replied. "But it does not say anything about triple nationality."

Holding multiple nationalities doesn't require extra patriotism; Kolomoisky, a Ukrainian nationalist, would never go to bat for Cyprus. Citizenship, in these cases, functions more as a Global Entry pass or an American Express card than a way of meaningfully identifying one's place in the world. It's no coincidence that a recent advertisement for Citibank describes its new credit card as "the new American passport."

The option of dissembling one's nationality is in fact what directly inspired Bashar Kiwan's deal with the Comoros. Friends and associates of Kiwan's told me that they, too, had considered seeking second citizenships or residence permits simply as a matter of course. Comorian lawmakers and Comoro Gulf Holding employees all pointed to established citizenship- and residence-by-investment programs in other countries as a sort of basis, or justification, for the Comorian law.

"Thank God there's this opportunity," Adnan Tarabishy, a Syrian media executive and acquaintance of Kiwan's, explained over Skype in February 2015. Tarabishy said he was in the process of applying for a passport from the island of Dominica to compensate for the inconvenience of being Syrian. "Market access is like a nightmare, so we consider this as part of our business investment," he told me.

There's a late-capitalist logic to the scheme. If citizenship can be freely bought and sold, why shouldn't governments buy them for stateless people?

Christian Kalin was born in 1971 in Zurich. As a teen, he enrolled in a pre-military service shooting program and spent his free time firing at imaginary enemies in the Swiss countryside. He also began collecting citizenship laws from different countries, writing to embassies to request copies of their legislation and keeping the documents in a big binder. "What always fascinated me was the inclusionary and exclusionary aspect of citizenship," Kalin told me over lunch one bright February afternoon on the island of Nevis. "I wanted to understand how different countries handled this."

Kalin ultimately decided that military life was not for him, and he obtained an exemption from service when studying abroad. He went to France, then to New Zealand, where he fell in love with a fellow student named Mae. He had trouble obtaining a proper permit that allowed him to stay in the country, so he "figured out how to work the system," as he puts it. Kalin extended his student visa by enrolling in more courses, and when Mae finished her studies, they moved to Switzerland, where Kalin enrolled in the University of Zurich to earn a Master of Laws.

While he was completing his degree in 1996, Kalin began

76 consulting for the company that he would eventually chair. Henley & Partners was then a small firm, and the relocation industry was only just emerging. The end of colonialism created a kind of citizenship anxiety. For example, people in the British colony of Hong Kong started to worry about China resuming control in 1997, particularly after witnessing the brutal crackdown over pro-democracy protests in Beijing's Tiananmen Square in the summer of 1989. (British officials, on their part, floated a half-baked plan to relocate some five million Hong Kongers to Northern Ireland.) Canada began offering residence permits to wealthy Hong Kongers and other foreigners, both big and small, soon passed their own versions of investor-immigration legislation programs. The Pacific islands of Tonga, Samoa, the Marshall Islands, Vanuatu, and Nauru set up decidedly shady schemes that apparently brought in a combined $152 million from mostly Chinese buyers looking for an "exit" or "tax passport" between 1982 and 1997. The U.S. Congress passed the Immigration Act of 1990, which included the EB-5 visa program, effectively selling permanent residence, or so-called green cards, to foreigners willing to invest at least half a million dollars in the U.S. In 2014, the program reached its yearly capacity of 10,000 permits for the first time; 85 percent of demand came from China. Since 2009, the overall number of applicants has almost doubled each year.

The fundamental concept of letting people "buy their way" into a country was politically fraught from the start. Don Myatt, who ran the immigrant investor scheme in Canada for ten years before moving to Antigua in 2012 to help the Caribbean state sell its citizenship, recalls that those in favor of putting a price tag

on being Canadian were made out to have "monster horns." The
concept continues to be contentious in North America, though
the conversation has evolved somewhat; the legal scholar Eric
Posner, for example, characterized the American EB-5 scheme
in a recent article for Slate as "ludicrous"—not because it was
unethical, but because the price tag was "extraordinarily low."

In the 1990s and early 2000s, Henley and a few competitors
ran small but successful ventures helping businessmen move
their money and families around the world. Henley became a
specialist in a Swiss tax break known as "forfait," which allows
rich foreign residents to negotiate lump-sum tax payments
based on their annual living expenses rather than their income
or assets. Henley also dabbled in procuring Caribbean passports for these wealthy clients; St. Kitts and Nevis had been
selling them since 1984, and the Commonwealth of Dominica
since 1990.

The Federation of St. Kitts and Nevis is the newest and, by
area and population, the smallest sovereign state in the Americas.
About 50,000 people live on the two islands in the northern
Lesser Antilles, and its shabby capital, Basseterre, sits just a few
miles from a large inactive volcano. St. Kitts housed the first
British and French colonies in the Caribbean and was known
as "The Mother Colony of the West Indies." Like the Comoro
Islands, it was used as a hub for the slave trade, and in 1983 it
declared independence from the British. At independence, St.
Kitts had little with which to support itself save for sugar exports;
it was essentially a Caribbean backwater.

In 1984, the islands added a citizenship-by-investment
provision to their naturalization act, opening the doors to

foreigners who made a "significant contribution" to the state. It seemed like an easy way to attract the occasional entrepreneur in the market for warmer climes and lower taxes. But the program lay practically dormant for twenty years, with only a couple hundred passports exchanged for investments in real estate during that time.

In 2006, just as the government was shutting down the failing sugar industry, Kalin arrived on the scene and proposed restructuring the passport program. He advised the government to create a fund for retraining former sugar workers, into which investors could directly donate $200,000 and qualify for citizenship. There would be a three-month wait, but investors wouldn't have to visit the islands—this was key for the small super-rich subset that considers travel to the Caribbean a dreadful inconvenience. He also told officials to make it easier for foreigners who purchase properties on the islands to receive citizenship as a perk. Finally, since few people had heard of St. Kitts and Nevis, the government should invest in marketing.

Prime Minister Denzil Douglas took well to Henley's plan. "At first, the prime minister wanted to know if these guys were for real," recalls Wendell Lawrence, who did double duty as a St. Kitts and Nevis ambassador and as Henley's man on the ground. "He eventually went to Switzerland on other business and paid Henley a visit in their offices in Zurich. That's when he decided to pursue their proposal."

With the go-ahead from the government, Henley was given exclusive rights to market the islands and their passport at conferences, panels, and events abroad—a concession that rankled their competitors. "Henley got really lucky," says

Nuri Katz, a Russian-Israeli American-Antiguan-Kittitian real-estate investor who is a frequent critic of Kalin. "Henley was nobody six years ago—they barely existed. Henley *is* Chris Kalin. He went to St. Kitts at the right time and the right place and said, 'Nobody is promoting this product. You're not getting clients, let me try to promote it for you.'"

Kalin and Lawrence took the St. Kitts and Nevis show on the road in 2006. They went door-to-door to pitch bankers and lawyers in Switzerland, Canada, and Singapore on the merits of Kittitian citizenship. Kalin worked with an obsessive, cerebral drive. "From the first time I met Chris, I could tell he was passionate about passports," Lawrence says. "It goes far beyond work. I could never understand it—it must be something personal. He was always going on about some book he'd read."

The men got off to a good start. HSBC, which offered clients relocation services, listed St. Kitts next to Canada, the United States, and the United Kingdom as possible options for expatriation, Lawrence recalls. Henley also teamed up with developers to sell property, earning commissions for citizenships sold through the real estate option. The company received $20,000 for every individual contribution into the so-called Sugar Industry Diversification Fund, whose website Henley actually registered out of its office on the island of Jersey off the coast of Normandy. Lawrence says the money was in lieu of marketing fees, which the government could not afford to pay otherwise.

A St. Kitts and Nevis passport got a lot more desirable in 2009, when holders were granted visa-free access to the Schengen Area, comprising 26 European countries. Kalin takes credit for this development; he says he successfully lobbied

European Union lawmakers. Suddenly, a Kittitian passport could be presented to Chinese or Russian businessmen as a must-have. St. Kitts became the breakthrough for Kalin. "We put St. Kitts on the map," Kalin says. "When you market Canada, you don't have to explain what Canada is—it has a brand. But you have to educate people about what St. Kitts and Nevis is. We positioned St. Kitts and Nevis as a viable product." "The amount of work that went into getting it off the ground was tremendous," Lawrence says. "I'm getting divorced now. I'd blame the travel from the citizenship-by-investment program. My marriage never recovered from it."

For St. Kitts, though, the union with Henley proved to be an economic miracle. In 2006, "passport money" accounted for about one percent of the country's GDP; by 2014, it hit 25 percent, with almost half of that amount coming from Sugar Industry Diversification Fund contributions (it's notable that this figure doesn't take into account the economic activity spurred by new construction). Passports are now the country's biggest export: The citizenship processing fees alone, which amount to $50,000 per applicant, have accounted on average for 7 percent of the country's annual GDP over the past five years. By comparison, the islands' manufacturing industry hovers at around 5 percent, economists at the St. Kitts-headquartered Eastern Caribbean Central Bank told me. Citizenship has enabled the country to pull itself out of an economic recession, increase bank liquidity, and balance its budget.

The effects are visible on the ground. The big hotel chains—Marriott, Four Seasons, Hyatt—collectively employ thousands of people to tend to the facilities. All over tiny St.

Kitts, new housing developments are cropping up, promising quick citizenship and 5 percent returns on rental income. The properties range from homogenous white blocks, built cheaply and quickly to ride the passport wave, to high-end resorts like Christophe Harbor, a sprawling luxury development on the southeastern side of the island. There, you can become Kittitian by buying into a share of a villa worth $400,000, which entitles you to several weeks occupancy; or by purchasing plots of land and holding on to them for at least five years, at which point you can re-sell the land (with a fresh passport attached) to someone else. And if your mega yacht happens to be pining for a new port, you can obtain citizenship by buying a marina berth. (Price tag: $1.5 to $3 million.) In downtown Basseterre, even abandoned lots come with seductive offers: "13050 Sq. Ft; Duty Free, Citizenship by Investment, and other Concessions apply," read a sign on a yellow shed not far from the port.

"All of this is thanks to our program," Kalin says, nodding toward the direction of construction projects as he drove very fast in his graphite Toyota Forerunner along roads devoid of other cars or even traffic lights, passing goats and the occasional horse or donkey.

"The rest of the Caribbean is totally broke. The impact of this program is really significant—the Caribbean is struggling, but St. Kitts is thriving."

Kalin is known as an aggressive businessman. His manner is direct, accountant-like, almost; he speaks in excellent Swiss German-accented English, stumbling over the occasional idiom but switching effortlessly between subjects ranging

82   from neoclassical economics to the Peace of Westphalia. His colleagues and acquaintances describe him as brilliant, impenetrable, and a little arrogant.

His attitude seems at least partly justified: The IMF, which helped the country restructure its debt, has taken note of the country's progress. "In St. Kitts and Nevis, the inflows into the real estate sector are fueling a construction boom, which has pulled the economy out of a four-year recession," states a report published in early 2015.

For his efforts, St. Kitts and Nevis made Kalin the country's honorary consul to Switzerland, and a special envoy on visa policy.

The transformation of St. Kitts came so suddenly and unexpectedly that observers, skeptical of the durability of the boom, speak of a "passport bubble." Cheap property developments, given the go-ahead by the cash-hungry government in order to attach passports to their stock, are over-valued, because the minimum investment for a foreign national to qualify as a Kittitian citizen is $400,000.

"It's a textbook real-estate bubble," says Thomas Liepman, the American manager of Christophe Harbor. "What happens in ten years when there are 2,000 'luxury' priced one-bedrooms or studio apartments and no one to rent them? People make below-poverty wages here. The rental market doesn't exist. . . . For a lot of developers it's a race against the clock: Let's get this built on cheap and easy financing, on the backs of citizenship investors, and then we'll have a fancy hotel." As for Christophe Harbor, Liepman insists that his clientele are interested in St.

Kitts more as an investment and vacation spot than as a proxy to obtain passports. "We joke that there's life in Christophe Harbor after citizenship."

The impact of passport sales in St. Kitts made waves in the normally placid Eastern Caribbean waters. Kalin suddenly had the ear of almost every politician in the region, with the notable exception of the president of St. Vincent and the Grenadines, who has loudly and publicly denounced the idea of selling citizenship, saying he has a "fundamental, philosophical objection" to the concept. These programs, critics argue, undermine the sense of community that ties a country's people together; they're also unfair because they give the rich opportunities and rights unavailable to everyone else.

"He's an old far-leftist," Kalin shrugged, referrering to the Caribbean leader. "He'll never be convinced." I met with Kalin in St. Kitts one evening after the country held elections. His phones were ringing off the hook. "We've been working with them for so long that we know where everything is and how everything works," he told me, excusing himself to take yet another call from a future or former official. "When the new cabinet can't find something, they call us."

Kalin may well have turned himself into a king—or, as some of his critics contend, a pirate of the Caribbean. He's built a lucrative business for his firm, and St. Kitts seems to have turned its fortunes around for the moment.

But for Kalin, his biggest triumph has been in turning a shady, fly-by-night business—hitherto the stuff of Bond villains and drug-trafficking rings—into not just an unlikely compliance tool, but a necessity for the business-class lounge set: according to Bloomberg, investor-citizens spent $2 billion buying passports in 2014.

Kalin spent last winter jetting around the Caribbean and completing his doctoral dissertation for the University of Zurich on the subject of citizenship by investment. Evidence of his academic endeavors can be found neatly stacked all over his living room: a paper by the Marxist philosopher Etienne Balibar here, books on European nationality policy there. And when he breaks down the geopolitical trends that drive Henley's business, he sounds more like a university professor than an executive; he has found in his work not just a lucrative business, but an intellectual calling. He notices a cultural sea change in the way countries and citizens conceive of the social contract, arguing that traditional ways of allocating citizenship to individuals—by birth or through blood—are fundamentally arbitrary: After all, you don't choose where you're born or who your parents are. Since we live in a globalized world, he says, birthplace and blood no longer hold the same significance as they used to.

"In modern times, we've gone from a territorial conception of citizenship, or *jus soli*, to one tied to heritage or blood—*jus sanguinis*. Now we're starting to see citizenship allocated in exchange for contributions to a state," he says. These contributions include money, of course—either received directly from the individual, or in the case of the Comoros, from another government—but also sporting ability, entrepreneurial skills, and other talents.

Kalin contends that investment-based citizenship may actually be *more* fair, because it makes more sense than randomly assigning privileged status by chance. "Of course it's only for the wealthy, but that's not any more of an arbitrary criteria [sic] than any other that we currently use to allocate citizenship," Kalin said. "If you can fulfill those criteria you can become a citizen."

By marketing passports like merchandise, the citizenship business has eroded a moral veneer that, for the past hundred years or so in the West, has come part and parcel with being of a place. What Kalin calls "access rights" to countries has become transactional, and the idea has even seeped onto the airwaves. "I fly like paper, get high like planes / If you catch me at the border I got visas in my name," the rapper M.I.A. bragged on the 2007 hit "Paper Planes." On the 2011 song "Otis," a collaboration between rappers Jay-Z and Kanye West, Jay-Z proudly declares, "Political asylum refugee can be purchased / Everything's for sale / I got five passports / I'm never going to jail."

After sealing the deal with St. Kitts, Kalin started island-hopping, advising the governments of Antigua, St. Lucia, and Grenada on how they could develop their own passport schemes. When the Mediterranean island nation of Malta put out a tender for consultants in 2013, Kalin won the right to help design its citizenship-by-investment program—it was Henley's biggest coup to date, since it concerned a member of the European Union. In less than five years, selling passports had turned into a veritable industry.

"They've taken an idea and moved it up a notch," says Don Myatt. "They made it a corporation. It has all the structure and pertinence as a normal business." Having left the Canadian

86   program behind, Myatt now runs Antigua's citizenship-by-investment unit out of an office building in downtown St.John, Antigua's capital, and does business with Kalin on a regular basis.

Myatt characterizes Henley's approach as conscientiously professional. "He knows that reputation is absolutely critical," he told me. "He wouldn't jeopardize it by doing business with dodgy characters." This was a crucial part of Kalin's strategy, since the underworld never lurks too far from the surface in these parts: A 2006 diplomatic cable notes that Dominican authorities had "taken criticism in the past for failing to adequately screen those to whom it grants economic citizenship, which is often sought by individuals attempting to avoid financial obligations or even criminal charges." Grenada shut down its first attempt at a passports-for-cash scheme shortly after the September 11 attacks (it has since been re-opened), and Ireland did the same to its own short-lived, below-the-radar variant in 1998 because politicians contended that it was not contributing enough to the Irish economy to justify the risks. Montenegro ran a scheme that drew criticism after the former Thai prime minister Thaksin Shinawatra, who was overthrown in a military coup, resurfaced as a Montenegrin citizen in 2010 (he was previously seen traveling with diplomatic Nicaraguan credentials). Montenegro's finance minister told the Financial Times that the billionaire head of state "gained his passport through a special decision because of investment promises."

Countries cannot technically prevent other nations from selling their citizenships, because naturalization is a fundamental part of state sovereignty. This legal question surfaced in 2014, after Henley designed its program for Malta. The European Commission, egged on by the outraged Maltese opposition party, held a debate on whether it was permissible for one of its members to sell off access to the entire Eurozone—with an EU passport, qualified investors could just as easily live in Berlin or Rome as they could in Valletta, Malta's capital. "It is legitimate to question whether EU citizenship rights should merely depend on the size of someone's wallet or bank account," the EU justice commissioner Viviane Reding said at the time.

Popular opinion, in Malta and in the Commission, was against Kalin's plan: During a meeting in January 2014, European Commission representatives voted to oppose the sale of citizenship in the EU by a margin of 560 to 22, with 44 abstentions. The Maltese sent their attorney general, accompanied by Kalin and a law professor named Dimitry Kochenov, to argue that the supranational body had no basis from which to regulate the naturalization policies of sovereign states. "Under EU law it's clear that the EU has no standing," Kochenov, a legal scholar at the University of Groningen, told me. "It was a political compromise." (Kochenov is Dutch, but he was born Russian; he says he appreciates the work Chris Kalin is doing "because the whole idea of assigning people to places is feudalism and anarchy.")

Malta also added a residence requirement of one year to the conditions—ostensibly to prove that these new Maltese could demonstrate a genuine link to their so-called nation—and the EU backed down. But even that requirement is ambiguous; investor-citizens can meet it by renting an apartment for twelve months. "They come twice, once to get a residency card and once to get a passport," a local lawyer told the *New York Times*.

As of July 2015, Henley said it represented 100 of the 140 applicants who have been approved for citizenship. The firm earned a 4 percent commission on each citizenship sold.

Other countries can retaliate against citizenship-selling nations by other means. This happened to St. Kitts in October 2013, when the U.S. Treasury's Financial Crimes Enforcement Network released a statement on "illicit actors"—including some Iranians—obtaining citizenship from St. Kitts to evade sanctions. The Canadian government also removed St. Kitts and Nevis from the list of countries whose citizens can travel to Canada visa-free.

These retaliations are of great concern to Kalin: Visa restrictions and other sanctions effectively lower the value of the passports on the market, which means fewer clients, decreased revenue, and a reputational risk that can jeopardize not just the program of one country, but the entire passport industry. "The underlying asset generating such inflows is the visa free access/ residency rights granted to foreign investors through the program [so] a change of visa policy in advanced economies is a significant risk," the IMF noted. "That can suddenly diminish the appeal of these programs and . . . even suspend their operation. Increasing competition from similar programs in other countries or a decline in demand from source countries can also rapidly reduce the number of applicants."

Kalin blames a rash of irresponsible competitors for the increased scrutiny on these programs. "The aim is to keep out the bozos," he told me. "Do you know what the definition of a bozo is? It's a stupid, incompetent person. They make us all look

bad." Kalin's "bozos" are hard to miss these days. CS Global, a
firm run by a former Henley employee named Micha-Rose
Emmett, is financed by one Dev Bath, the flamboyant son of
an Indian industrialist; the pair took out a 12-page advertising supplement in the *Financial Times* last October entitled,
simply, "Belong."

"Introducing the oldest and most trusted citizenship by
investment programs in the world," the cover reads, above a
photo of a woman in a zebra-striped bikini reclining on the back
of a speedboat. "Discover the benefits of becoming a citizen of
the world." The leaflet advertises the Dominican and Kittitian
programs as well as the firm's executives. "I became a citizen of
St. Kitts and Nevis and Dominica over ten years ago," Bath's tes-
timonial says, below a photograph of him wearing jeans and a
white suit jacket with gold military tassels as he stands in the
mezzanine of what appears to be a dimly lit casino. "I know the
benefits supported the needs of my family and my business."

"Globalization is a reality," adds Emmett, on the facing page.
The company now works with St. Kitts and Nevis under a contract similar to the one Henley struck with the Douglas administration in 2005.

Arton Capital, a Dubai-based consultancy firm, is another
big name that's giving Kalin a run for his money. The company
is run by a smooth-talking Armenian-Canadian-Dominican-
Antiguan-Comorian named Armand Arton, who says he buys
passports from the countries he works with out of sheer principle. "I'm working toward getting ten," he told me one night over
drinks at the St. Regis Hotel in New York, in a room milling with
UN General Assembly attendees. "I want to be in the *Guinness*

90 *Book of World Records."*

Arton, the son of Armenian immigrants who was recently appointed a special envoy to Antigua and Barbuda, got his start helping Iranians and other Middle Easterners move to Canada under the country's investor immigration program. He then moved to Dubai and started his own firm, which does similar work to Henley but relies more heavily on contract agents working in each region.

Arton's pet project is selling Bulgarian papers. In 2014, a *Daily Telegraph* journalist went undercover and was told by one of Arton's representatives that it would be possible to obtain Bulgarian papers for as little as 180,000 Euros even if the applicant had had prior run-ins with the law. But marketing is Arton Capital's biggest talent: the firm is known for building a flashy website, producing globe-themed party favors, including a leaflet shaped like a passport with every citizenship-by-investment option inside and a name tag that looks like a boarding pass, hiring models to staff his events, and parking Arton-branded race cars outside conference hotel entrances, just for show.

Though Arton lacks Swiss discretion, he's still taking cues from Henley. Both Kalin and Arton have courted the same names—academics, thought leaders, researchers, heads of state—to speak at their conferences. Both men are organizing their own respective "Global Citizen Awards" to honor an individual who represents the greatest hope for global citizenship. (The Clinton Global Initiative has an eponymous award; among its honorees are Malala Yousefsai, former New York City mayor Mike Bloomberg, and the CEO of a bakery known as the "United

Nations of Bread.") Both firms publish a ranking of the best and worst passports—Arton successfully one-upped Henley's list in 2015 with a slick infographic that made the rounds on design blogs—and have recently brought in speakers from international institutions to further legitimize their business.

No existing international body would have the authority to govern the citizenship laws of sovereign states to begin with, but both firms are also concerned with how to keep external regulators out of the industry. Last October, Arton announced that he was forming an industry group to ensure that citizenship-by-investment programs properly benefited the countries they served. The same day, Kalin launched his Investment Migration Council, a nonprofit chaired in Geneva which aims to do the same thing. "It's like kindergarteners," remarks Kim Marsh, a frequent guest at both company's events who works for a due diligence company called IPSA.

The men are fighting over market dominance, but also over whose company appears to be the best "global citizen." In early 2015, Kalin announced that Henley had partnered with the UN Refugee Agency to help those "at the other end of the spectrum of global mobility"—actual stateless people and displaced persons, as opposed to denizens of Davos. Arton has a more creative plan. "I had a thought that for every passport we sell, we should donate one to a stateless person," Arton told me. What capitalism can do for shoes, capitalism can do for passports, too.

In fact, philanthropy was the unofficial theme at Arton's 2014 "Global Citizenship Forum" in Toronto. (Henley has put on its own Global Citizenship and Residence conferences since 2006.) There were presentations about how to buy a passport, of course, but there was also a fair amount of soul-searching about the "responsibilities" of global citizens.

On the second day of talks, a gargantuan red-headed heir to the Swiss Nestlé fortune named Patrick Liotard-Vogt gave a heartfelt speech about his view of what global citizens owe the world. Vogt, a Swiss-Kittitian and an alum of the world's most expensive boarding schools in the Alps, recently became the chairman of A Small World, a kind of Myspace for jet-set-ters—a socialite network, basically. "For the past few hours and days we've been talking about global citizens," he began. "We've learned they're ultra-high-net-worth individuals, they're well traveled, they're entrepreneurs, they have families, they have higher educations. They have it all. They are literally almost supernatural. But there's one thing I think we shouldn't forget," Vogt continued. "They're also just human beings. We talk about them like data, but they're human beings, they have interests, they have passions. And we've kind of missed that topic.

"Economic citizens have no connection to the country. I just crossed the border with my St. Kitts passport in Zurich and the guy at the booth said, 'Oh, that's funny—there was a guy three hours ago who passed through here on one of those, and I asked him where St. Kitts was, and he didn't know.' My wish as a global citizen is to appeal to you to have a more meaningful experience with that passport. The governments should create an identity for their country and market that. If we have proud and happy citizens there's more opportunity for investment than just the passport."

The conference ended on this pensive note, and at night-fall the festivities began. Wine flowed; steak was served; a gaudy variety show stretched well into the night. There were traditional Caribbean dancers and performers from Cirque du Soleil. The motivational speaker Robin Sharma made the audience give each other hugs; the comedian Russell Peters made fun of Antiguan prime minister Gaston Browne's "Hitler mustache" and roasted the attendees for being stateless. "What you are, sir, is a man with no home," he pointed at Armand Arton. "You are the most successful homeless guy ever."

Then, an aggressively multicultural choir took the stage and gave a heartfelt rendition of "We Are the World," the fast-est-selling American pop single in history when it was released in 1985, co-written by Michael Jackson and Lionel Richie, and performed by Bob Dylan, Tina Turner, Ray Charles, and doz-ens of other artists.

"We are all a part of God's great big family," the children bellowed.

A piano flourish took the group into a heavily harmonized chorus.

"It's true we'll make a better day, just you and me."

As the pianist put the finishing notes on the song, the crowd erupted in applause. Several members of the audience looked a little weepy.

We Are the World

"In this world, shipmates, sin that pays its way can travel freely, and without a passport, whereas Virtue, if a pauper, is stopped at all frontiers."

—Herman Melville, *Moby Dick*

In 1863, the *Atlantic Monthly* published a short story dramatizing the life of a fictional American Army lieutenant named Philip Nolan. Nolan renounces his citizenship in a fit of anger during a trial for treason; the judge sentences him to spend the rest of his days at sea, floating from ship to ship, without any news from nor mention of his homeland.

Nolan leaves defiantly, but over time, he misses America more than he misses his family, his friends, or even the touch of dry land. On his deathbed, Nolan lets an officer into his room—a "shrine to patriotism"—and asks for news of his country, which the officer recounts to him as he lies dying.

Edward Everett Hale's "The Man Without a Country" is a 95 cautionary tale: Be true to your country, or endure a lifetime of pain and exile. Defection from the motherland is presented as a supreme moral failing. Statelessness as tragedy—a fate worse than death.

But less than a century after Hale's story was published, the narrative of the man without a country was rewritten, this time in real life. To this day, the reasons why individuals renounce their citizenship speak volumes about the times in which they live.

On May 25, 1948, a 26-year-old American veteran named Garry Davis walked into the U.S. embassy in Paris, renounced his American citizenship, and declared himself a citizen of the world.

Davis wasn't dodging a draft, or defecting to Russia. He had fought in the Second World War and had nothing against America in particular; in fact, the country had treated him well. The son of Meyer Davis, a bandleader who ran several orchestras that played clubs, weddings, and high-society balls, Garry grew up among show business celebrities and rode to school in a limousine. At the time of his draft, he was studying acting at the Carnegie Institute of Technology and had the start of a promising career; he'd played the understudy to Danny Kaye in the Cole Porter musical *Let's Face It* and took over one night when the actor was ill with laryngitis. "There were fan letters, a Columbia screen test offer, and feelers for the lead in a comedy planned for the next season," Davis wrote. "My stage career had seemed assumed except for the fact that I was later drafted."

In 1940, he took off to serve his country and became a pilot, participating in missions that included flying over Brandenburg in a B-17 and dropping bombs on the cities below. His brother, Bud, was killed in action in 1944 at Salerno, "his old tub of a destroyer blown to Kingdom Come in the early hours of the invasion," as Davis remembered it. Davis, grieving, "prayed for a chance to exact revenge."

During a particularly harrowing mission called the Peenemünde raid, which was intended to disable secret German weapons development facilities, Davis and his co-pilot crash-landed in Sweden. They were discharged shortly thereafter. Despite not having settled the score with his brother's killers, the pilot's conscience began to eat at him. "I began to question the morality of punishing the German people with our superior firepower," Davis wrote in the first of his seven books, *My Country Is the World*. "How many bombs had I dropped? How many men, women, and children had I murdered? Wasn't there another way, I kept asking myself."

In 1944, Davis returned home and tried to pick up the pieces of his acting career. Instead of a rising Broadway star, he felt, in his words, like a "sad clown." He worried that the peace he fought for would eventually deteriorate again into a Third World War, and he was disappointed with the newly formed United Nations, which "seemed to have been still-born, a glorified *Kaffeeklatsch* incapable of solving major problems."

It began to dawn on him that nationalism, not human nature, was responsible for the bloodshed that had taken place, and it might be better if the world's people weren't divided into categories determined by arbitrary lines based on historical accidents. Some 2,500 years earlier, Zeno and the Stoics had said that moral evolution required rising above national borders and joining a universal community. After his experience in a devastating war, Davis came to the same conclusion.

A young Harvard graduate named Henry Martyn Noel had given up his papers in 1947 and gone to Germany to repair a bombed-out church; Davis read about Noel in the *New York Times* and was inspired to follow his lead. He began imagining a world government that would bring people together, not tear them apart. "It's the oldest idea in the world—it goes back to ancient Greece," Davis told me in 2012. "They call themselves cosmopolites. Socrates, 2,500 years ago, said, 'Don't call yourself just an Athenian, or a Greek—call yourself a citizen of the world.'" He decided that he would be its first formal citizen.

First, though, he had to give up his American passport.

The U.S. Nationality Act requires Americans to be on foreign soil before renouncing ties with their homeland. So Davis, like so many disenchanted Americans before him, went to Paris. At the U.S. embassy on the Place de la Concorde, he explained his motives to the befuddled consul, swore that he was fully aware of what he was doing on a Bible he borrowed from a nearby hotel, and left the embassy as a man without a country.

"As I walked out of the Embassy into the little court, I sensed a strange freedom," he wrote in his memoir. He saw two Marines standing outside the building carrying sidearms, "as if they belonged in the Middle Ages," and he felt a little sorry for them. "I'm still me. The only thing that changed is I was one passport lighter," Davis said. "I slept that night quite illegally."

Davis quickly learned what millions of stateless people around the world know all too well: Without papers, he was legally not allowed to remain in France, and he couldn't go anywhere else, either. He was given a residence permit for three months, but he threw it in the trash, because documents "give status, dignity, and privilege to the issuing authority rather than to the bearer." When his permit expired and was not renewed, he fashioned a World Citizen International Identity Card out of cardboard. He was citizen number one.

Davis wasn't done with theatrics yet; the Broadway show of his life was only beginning. In the autumn, the United Nations General Assembly came to town for three months. Its offices at the Palais de Chaillot became international territory, and Davis was still essentially itinerant. It was too good a chance to pass up. What better home could there be for a citizen of the world?

On September 12, Davis settled in the United Nations restaurant—the only part of the establishment that would let him through the doors. He had with him just a Bible, a typewriter, and the clothes he wore.

The press loved him, and for good reason: The story of Garry Davis was also the story of the century. Europe was still settling into the borders that decades of conflict had torn up, scattered, and reset repeatedly, creating millions of refugees. And because of the wars, passport controls had become more stringent, putting those without valid travel documents in the difficult position of being told to go home, but having no safe home to go back to.

An early solution to the problem of stateless people traveling had been the "Nansen" passport, conceived by Fritjof

Nansen, a Norwegian statesman and explorer who served as the UN's High Commissioner for Refugees in the 1920s. His initial mandate was to figure out what to do with the large number of White Russian refugees who'd fled their country after the 1917 revolution and had their citizenship taken away under a 1922 denationalization decree. Nansen suggested a sort of supranational alternative to a passport, which allowed displaced and/or stateless persons to emigrate and travel. Representatives from sixteen governments signed on to the treaty on July 5, 1922, and by the end of the decade more than fifty countries accepted the passports as valid proof of identification. "The emergence of the Nansen Passport was a striking demonstration of how rising nationalism and ideological conflict could prompt more intensive internationalism," writes Mark Mazower in *Governing the World*, a history of international organizations. "As new nation-states introduced citizenship laws that excluded minorities or (in the Russian case) political opponents, people were stranded by the fortunes of war, possessing only temporary papers or a birth certificate issued by some now-defunct empire. The Nansen Passport offered one way around this new problem and eventually some 450,000 of them were issued."

They don't make statesmen like Nansen anymore: a consummate polymath who also earned a PhD in zoology and made exploratory trips to the North Pole, he won the Nobel Prize in 1922 for his humanitarian work. His legacy endures. Notable Nansen passport holders included Vladimir Nabokov, Igor Stravinsky, and Ivan Soboleff, a White Russian Cossack officer who quit his regiment in Chinese Turkestan, then traveled around the world by bicycle and motorbike for two years.

He wrote a book, *Nansen Passport*, about his adventures. (Soboleff's exploits recall the old Prussian term for the passport: *Wanderbuch*.)

Around this time, the use of national passports had become commonplace in the West. National IDs had been issued to citizens by governments for close to two centuries, though often to place limits on peoples' comings and goings rather than allow them to move more freely. In *The Invention of the Passport*, John Torpey, a professor of sociology and history at the Graduate Center of the City University of New York, characterizes the emergence of the early passport regime as a process wherein people "become dependent on states for the possession of an 'identity' from which they can escape only with difficulty and which may significantly shape their access to various spaces."

In revolutionary France, the concept of making people carry an identification document was incredibly controversial. When lawmakers began debating the matter, one outspoken critic said that "a nation that claims to have a constitution cannot enchain the liberty of its citizens to the extent that you propose. A revolution that commenced with the destruction of passports must insure a sufficient measure of freedom to travel, even in times of crisis."

Torpey notes that countries began to define themselves not just culturally, politically, or militarily, but administratively, too. "The emergence of passport and related controls on movement is an essential aspect of the 'state-ness' of states," he wrote.

It was not until the First World War broke out that ordinary national passports were used on a massive scale, according to Mazower. In 1920, the League of Nations met to standardize passports, a convention that spoke to the growing importance of the documents. So the timing of Nansen's initiative was significant: at a time when nationalist fevers were running high, the concept of a supranational document was a revolutionary one.

That wasn't enough for Garry Davis, though. The League of Nations and its successor, the United Nations, were in no way committed to ending state sovereignty, and Davis believed that humans should belong to a bigger, more inclusive, almost universal community. This brand of cosmopolitanism was in vogue: Luminaries such as Albert Einstein (who was once stateless), Albert Camus, and Buckminster Fuller began advocating for some variant on a world government. In the United States, World Federalist movements were cropping up and joining forces, hoping to unite humanity to prevent another war. The *New Yorker* published an editorial in its June 5, 1948 issue about Davis: "renouncing US citizenship in order to become a citizen of the world is an exciting gesture." Still, it went on to say that "a man without a country is not in a good position to embrace the planet; he is too busy answering questions." The *Montreal Gazette* said that Davis "is making rather more of an impact on the world than was generally anticipated." Other outlets were just as curious, if less sympathetic; *Pravda* called him "a maniac exporting world government from America along with powdered eggs and detective stories," while the *New York Daily Mirror* accused him of being a Soviet spy.

Davis was, for lack of a better term, a ham. When the authorities tried to get him to leave the UN, he informed them that sending him out of international territory would be a violation of French law, since he was undocumented and had been denied a permit to stay in France. "But you are still in Paris," a policeman protested. "*Mais oui*," Davis replied. "This may still be Paris, but for the moment it is international Paris."

He remained in the UN for a week, holding court, making statements, and exchanging ideas with his growing audience. Old French ladies gave him tins of foie gras, bottles of wine, and packets of English biscuits. He received so much food and clothing that he donated it to charity. A hodgepodge of resistance activists, pacifists, and idealists gathered around the tent he eventually pitched on the restaurant patio, asking questions and lending their support. Robert Sarrazac, a former French resistance fighter who shared his views, introduced him to Albert Camus, André Breton, and dozens of other prominent French intellectuals, who decided to make a statement together at a UN General Assembly meeting.

On November 19, Davis entered the assembly hall with Camus, Sarrazac, and some fifty other sympathizers, who'd brought cameras, film equipment, and audio recorders. Davis stood on a balcony waiting for a lull in the session, and when his cameraman made a sign, he jumped the railing and ran onto the podium. "Mr. Chairman and delegates, I interrupt in the name of the people of the world not represented here," Davis declared, ripping off his coat. The room fell silent. He felt a frog in his throat. "Pass the world to the people!" he shouted, forgetting the rest of the 45-second-long speech he had written. "One government for one world!" Security escorted him out and Sarrazac took over the podium, and their comrades carried on the show for half an hour. The next day, Davis was once again the talk of the town. In the coming months, hundreds of "World Citizen Clubs" formed around Europe Entire towns announced that they were "World Towns." Leaflets were dropped around Paris advocating for Davis's cause. He held press conferences regularly. In December, Sarrazac and his friends arranged for Davis to give speech to almost 20,000 people at the Vélodrome d'Hiver.

Davis became "the symbol of frontierlessness," in the 1940s. Once, he stole $47 worth of women's undergarments so that the French would put him in jail rather than deport him. Eventually he was sent back to the U.S., but soon he sailed to Le Havre as a stowaway on a ship, only to be intercepted by border guards; back in the U.S., he stood before a judge, "smiled in a fatherly way, sentenced me to a week in jail, suspended the sentence and released me in my own custody." On one sojourn he went to Afghanistan, Pakistan, Iran, and the Netherlands. Remarkably, he entered many of these countries with his homemade World Passport, although he frequently ended up behind bars. Each entry stamp and arrest served to further validate his status as a world citizen. He was photographed with Indian prime minister Jawaharlal Nehru. He exchanged letters with Eleanor Roosevelt and Albert Schweitzer.

Davis also formed the World Service Authority, a Washington-based organization now staffed mainly by idealistic interns and law students. The WSA says it's issued World Passports and ID cards to more than 2.5 million people who were willing to pay $45 and fill out a simple form. Some holders have successfully crossed borders using their documents; others depend on it as their only form of identification. I received a World Passport free of charge in 2012, but the only border I've crossed with it was the one between a street and the inside of a bar.

I first contacted Davis in 2011, when I was working on an article about Americans who give up their citizenship for tax reasons, and after several months of correspondence and phone calls I met him in the spring of 2012. (Davis had a tendency to call out of nowhere, just to chat.) He told me to come to the Sheraton hotel in midtown Manhattan—the same hotel where the Clinton Global Initiative would host their Global Citizen award the following year.

There was no fancy gala for Garry Davis that day. In fact, he didn't even have a room. I found him camped out in a corner of the lobby, surrounded by pamphlets, documents, bags, and a green-and-white World Citizen banner that he'd draped over a chair. "When I'm giving an interview, I always have to have the flag, because I'm sovereign," he greeted me. Unwashed, penniless, and 90 years old, he seemed to me a little tragic, sitting all by himself with his shabby propaganda spread out around him like a big, messy quilt—the emperor of a nation of one. He'd spent his entire life challenging what it meant to be a citizen of a country and promoting a more equitable and inclusive vision of humanity that crossed national, racial, political, and religious lines. By the beginning of the twenty-first century, his vision— which was not just acknowledged, but debated, even celebrated in the years after the war—became largely seen as untenable and eccentric. In this gleaming hotel, people who'd flown in from all over the world, passports still in their hands, surrounded this

Fisher King. No one seemed to notice he was there. Still, Davis was optimistic about the potential for technology to usher in a new era of world citizenship.

"What has happened in terms of technology and electronics is we've eliminated time and distance between people," he told me. "We're all there. We're all there! So that's a fact. For us to be governed by an eighteenth-century institution called a nation is obviously insane."

The next summer, in July 2013, Davis checked himself into a hospice in Burlington, Vermont, where he'd spent much of his life. He had married three times—once at sea—and fathered four children who hold Canadian, French, British, and U.S. citizenships, but he was estranged from all but one of them. He died six days later at the age of 91, just three days short of 92, and most of the major U.S papers ran obituaries recounting his adventures.

Davis was very much a product of his time: idealistic, shell-shocked, giddy about the possibility of a different, unified world. Darren O'Byrne, a professor of sociology and human rights at Roehampton University who knew Davis personally and wrote a chapter on him in an upcoming book on global citizenship entitled *Human Rights in a Globalizing World*, said that this unmediated engagement with the conditions in which he was living made Davis's version of global citizenship more practical and forward-thinking than utopian. "The Stoics said, 'I'm a citizen of the world,'" O'Byrne says. "But what they meant was, 'I identify with all my fellow humans or under God or as one people.' But in a globalized world, the impact of world events on your life is global. You have to engage politically, meaningfully, in ways that people of past generations didn't have to."

A younger activist might dismiss Davis's statements as out of touch, especially given how little Davis achieved in the way of ending nationalism. But it's crucial to consider the magnitude of the earth-shattering changes Davis was able to witness in real time over the course of his long life. Davis fought tiny battles at checkpoints just as air travel was becoming accessible to large numbers of people; he disseminated his message of world government during a time when landlines, fax machines, cell phones, and computers helped us to forget about the realities of distance, space, and time.

In the final decade of his life, Garry Davis saw non-state actors such as Al Qaeda force nations to redefine the ways they wage war. Organizations like WikiLeaks and Anonymous challenge these wars with troves upon troves of information. Looming environmental crises reveal the cracks in our system of international governance, and threaten the very existence of many countries as we know them.

Davis saw it all coming, and the world was his stage. Before tax-free zones, freeports, and airports became indispensable cogs in the machinery of globalization, Davis found ways to exploit them. It's essentially the same loophole that has allowed WikiLeaks founder Julian Assange to seek refuge at the Ecuadorean embassy in London, where, as of this writing, he languishes still. It's the tool Edward Snowden exploited during his stint living in Moscow's Sheremetyevo International Airport after he leaked National Security Agency data in a hotel in Hong Kong and went on the run.

Just weeks before his death, Davis appeared on CBS news
and announced that he had sent Snowden a World Passport.

When Roger Ver travels, he makes a point of wearing his favorite item of clothing: a green T-shirt with a globe and the phrase "borders are imaginary lines" silk-screened on the front.

But when I met Ver, the world's most vocal supporter of the crypto-currency Bitcoin, near his beachfront apartment at the Marriott hotel on St. Kitts last February, he was learning the hard way that however imaginary these lines might be in his mind, they matter a great deal in practice—even for a young white tech investor from California.

Ver was born American in 1979. He went shopping for a new passport after deciding he no longer wanted any associations with a country he considered violent, coercive, and immoral. After a false start that involved an online scammer, a trip to Guatemala, an illegitimate South American passport, and tens of thousands of dollars, Ver bought a St. Kitts and Nevis citizenship the honest way, and renounced his American papers in 2014.

One year later, he applied for a visa to come back for a Bitcoin conference in Miami. He assumed the U.S. would let him back in; it wasn't as though he intended to emigrate illegally, or come back to mooch off the state.

While there is a provision in a 1996 law that allows U.S. authorities to bar certain renouncers from returning, Ver's visitor visa was rejected on the grounds that he could not prove he wasn't planning on moving back for good. He reapplied, with additional evidence, twice; the embassy rejected him both times.

"Do you really think I want to move back to the U.S.?" Ver asked me angrily. "I can't believe anyone would accuse me of wanting to move back."

The rejection stung particularly hard because of Ver's politics and vocation. Though he is no longer a U.S. citizen on paper, he retains a distinctly American obsession with personal freedom; he spends much of his time jetting to conferences, where he proselytizes about the revolutionary potential of Bitcoin to free us from borders, governments, and what Garry Davis described as "the cavernous, bureaucratic, subhuman passageway of dots and curlicues, lorded over by rubber stamps."

On the other hand, the string of denials shouldn't have been a complete surprise. Ver will be the first to admit that his relationship with the American authorities had been fraught throughout his entire adult life. In 2000, he became a libertarian candidate for the California State Assembly. His platform was refreshingly simple: "HUGE TAX CUTS. HUGE SPENDING CUTS. HUGE DECREASE IN NUMBER OF LAWS." He lost.

The previous year he had founded Memory Dealers, a successful online computer parts business, but in 2002 federal agents arrested him for selling explosives on the online auction site eBay. He was sentenced to 10 months in prison and subsequently "shut his mouth" when it came to politics, convinced that he had been targeted for voicing his anti-establishment views during his campaign. He spent much of the next decade living in Japan, a move inspired, he says, by dating a Japanese woman who had been living in America.

In 2011, Ver discovered and invested in the digital currency Bitcoin. It was a light-bulb moment for Ver, and his

enthusiasm for the project compelled him to speak out once $\quad$
more, authorities be damned. "Money without borders is a
world without borders," he repeats, over and over. "Bitcoin is
the future." It didn't hurt that Bitcoin, in addition to dovetail-
ing perfectly with his political views, made him a rich man: Ver
bought in when the currency was selling at around $1 per coin,
and before the year was up, its value soared, turning him into
a millionaire. When I met Ver in St. Kitts, he helped me set up
a virtual wallet for Bitcoin on my iPhone, and moments later,
sent me $20 worth of the currency. This amounted to less
than one-tenth of a Bitcoin; in February 2015, a single unit of
the currency was worth $240, down from a high of more than
$1,200 in 2013.

When he had the money, Ver did what he'd dreamed
of doing for years: he bought a new passport, renounced
his American citizenship, and became a full-time Bitcoin
propagandist. Ver didn't know much about Garry Davis, but
his reasons for leaving the U.S. were essentially political, too:
He did not want to support his native country in any way,
shape, or form, be it through allegiances or taxes. Like Davis,
Ver doesn't believe in national citizenship, which he finds
limiting and unfair; he feels his citizenship should be his, not
fate's (or Big Brother's), to choose.

Ver recalls the day he rid himself of his American associations as "one of the happiest moments in my life." His
only regret is that he didn't do it sooner. Still, he didn't make
himself stateless; the inconvenience would have been too great
for such a frequent flyer. In this respect, Ver, too, is a man of
his time.

Ver cuts a charismatic figure. Clean-shaved, fresh-faced, and often smiling, he stays trim thanks to regular Jujutsu training that he took up in Tokyo. "I didn't want to be the fat American," he told me, as he exchanged text messages with his coach on one of three smartphones and scarfed down plantains and oatmeal in anticipation of a strenuous training session.

Like missionaries of all stripes, Ver's enthusiasm is infectious, and his manner—conscientiously polite, almost mechanically considerate—serves his message of deliverance well. At 35, Ver represents a new spin on the rootless, no-allegiance global citizen. While Davis owed much of his position to the ideas circulating after the World Wars, Ver's ideas are rooted in a curious set of ideological beliefs that have gathered currency since the development of the tech sector in California and the freewheeling global capitalism that has since taken hold. As a libertarian, Ver thinks the world would be freer, happier, more peaceful, and more just if we all let the free market dictate who does what where, when, and how. His moral philosophy is based on self-ownership and enlightened self-interest; his nasal earnestness recalls an adolescent boy who has read Ayn Rand for the first time and cannot stand to keep the revolutionary potential of radical individualism to himself.

In advocating for better living through technology, Ver channels a bizarre brand of techno-utopianism that the writer Evgeny Morozov calls "solutionism," which Morozov defines as "an intellectual pathology that recognizes problems as problems based on just one criterion: whether they are 'solvable' with a nice and clean technological solution at our disposal."

These problems include funding infrastructure, making
medical research more efficient, and even death. Ver (who com-
ments constantly, and with great concern, on his age) is convinced
that in due course, we will be able to reverse aging, making us all
forever young. "Hopefully we'll eventually merge with cyborgs
and all become silicon based," he mused. "Because human
flesh is pretty weak. I would love to not eat or sleep or get tired
or grumpy."

He's even signed up for his body to be cryogenically fro-
zen after his death—and eventual rebirth. His boyish charm
belies what, in an older, less attractive man, would immediately reveal itself as a deep paranoia of the tinfoil-hat variety.

Besides zombies, the most fundamental problem that
technology can solve is the problem of borders, according to
Ver, because nations and their governments meddle with people's lives and prevent them from being truly free. And so it was
particularly insulting for him to be prevented from preaching
the gospel of Bitcoin at the conference in Miami because of
national borders and the whims of an American bureaucrat.
This is, after all, the man who's known as "Bitcoin Jesus."

"It didn't turn out so well for the real Jesus," Ver said as
he sounded off against the "tyrants." "He was murdered by his
government. I hope that doesn't happen to me."

Bitcoin is a decentralized digital payment system that is
entirely independent of, and unregulated by, banks. Created
in 2009 by someone using the pseudonym Satoshi Nakamoto,
Bitcoins are "mined" by computers that take records of previous transactions. The computers turn the records into code
and add them to a "blockchain," or a constantly evolving ledger

that's stored on every Bitcoin-holder's computer. That means that goods can be bought anonymously, without the transactions ever getting traced back to either the buyer or the seller. It also means money can be transferred internationally without any bank fees. Because it is a currency that exists only in computer code, Bitcoin has been vulnerable to easy theft and fraud, making its worth immensely volatile, and some economists have predicted that Bitcoins will soon be worth nothing. Nevertheless, Ver is still an unreserved evangelist. He is playing the long game, perhaps because he truly believes that he will live forever.

Ver sees in Bitcoin a future in which nation-states cannot regulate the commercial activities of individuals. "Bitcoin is the money of the world," he says. "It doesn't care about borders. It doesn't care about any of that. It doesn't even care if you're a human. Imagine!" On his website, Ver calls Bitcoin "the most important invention in the history of the world since the Internet."

If Garry Davis showed ordinary men and women that they could broaden their allegiances and consider caring about a world beyond their hometown or country, Ver's cohort talk a big game about transacting outside the confines of the state. Davis led small-town mayors to call their towns "world towns"; Ver's acolytes talk businesses around the world into accepting Bitcoin as a form of payment. Davis felt accountable to all humankind; his cosmopolitanism mirrored that of the Stoics, in that it was inclusive and universal. Ver, ever the Cynic, sees global citizenship as a way of opting out. Call it dismal cosmopolitanism.

It is impossible to talk about renouncing American citizenship without talking about money. That's not the case for most nationalities: the Internal Revenue Service is unique in that the agency requires all U.S. citizens, whether they live in Kentucky or Kathmandu, to file tax returns annually. Additionally, citizens and permanent residents must usually pay the difference between the local tax rate and the U.S. rate if they make more than $99,200 per year. (Other countries tax on the basis of residence, not nationality.) Renouncing citizenship is the only legal way to avoid doing so. As a committed libertarian, Ver openly dislikes the idea of paying taxes. But it doesn't take an ideologue, or even a tax cheat, for that matter, to get annoyed at the inconvenience of being a U.S. citizen abroad. As a result of an ongoing crackdown on tax evasion abroad that requires banks to report the activities of their American clients to the U.S. government, an increasing number of Americans are choosing to call it quits. Last year, the U.S. Treasury released a list of names showing that at least 3,415 Americans renounced, up from just a couple hundred in 2008. (Tax lawyers and *Forbes* blogger Robert W. Wood, who writes regularly on tax matters relating to expatriation, believe the "published name and shame list is invariably incomplete.") The demand has created a waiting list for renunciation interviews at embassies abroad.

Since the tax rate in many countries tends to be on par with, if not higher than, in the U.S., renouncing doesn't end up saving ordinary expats much money. A number of middle-class renouncers have told me that the relief of not having to deal with the IRS each year makes it worth the hassle; since

114   2010, Americans living abroad have had trouble opening bank accounts because the burden of reporting their transactions to the U.S. tax authorities under a new law called the Foreign Account Tax Compliance Act (FATCA) has become so great.

Expatriating for tax reasons isn't cheap and easy, either. There's a $2,350 fee, and all renouncers must show that they are current on their past tax bills. If their net worth exceeds $2 million, they must pay an "exit tax," based on how much their assets were worth on the open market the day before their expatriation. (When we spoke, Ver said he was still waiting to find out how much he was on the hook for.)

Giving up U.S. citizenship can nevertheless result in significant savings in the long run. In 2012, Facebook co-founder Eduardo Saverin was publicly upbraided when he was found to have defected to Singapore—which, like St. Kitts, has no capital gains tax—shortly before the social networking website announced its initial public offering. The *Wall Street Journal* estimated that he'd saved upwards of $700 million. Adding insult to injury was the fact that Saverin's family fled Brazil when he was a child to seek a better life in the U.S. His global, a la carte approach to citizenship, residence, and taxation flies in the face of a more traditional view of belonging, which entails lifelong rights and responsibilities.

"This is a great American success story gone wrong," New York senator Chuck Schumer said in a statement before introducing the Expatriation Prevention by Abolishing the Tax-Related Incentives for Offshore Tenancy Act, or Ex-PATRIOT. "Mr. Saverin wants to de-friend the United States just to avoid paying taxes, and we're not going to let him get away with it."

"I have paid and will continue to pay any taxes due on everything I earned while a U.S. citizen," Saverin responded at the time. "It is unfortunate that my personal choice has led to a public debate, based not on the facts but entirely on speculation and misinformation."

It's not a coincidence that Ver and Saverin are big names in the tech sector, an industry that is increasingly set on turning all commerce into a convenient, personalized service and "disrupting" traditional enterprise to be faster, cheaper, easier. Given these priorities, why wouldn't citizenship come next? Ver's cultural milieu of "solutionists" has emerged among today's most vocal and powerful proponents of a border-free world of global citizens. John Perry Barlow, a founder of the digital rights group Electronic Frontier Foundation and a lyricist for the Grateful Dead, warned governments of the world of their looming irrelevance in his Declaration of the Independence of Cyberspace, which was published online in 1996. "Governments of the Industrial World, you weary giants of flesh and steel, I come from Cyberspace, the new home of Mind," Barlow typed from a computer in Davos, Switzerland. "I declare the global social space we are building to be naturally independent of the tyrannies you seek to impose on us."

Today, you won't find Barlow's heirs camped out on the steps of the UN, and you certainly won't hear them singing "We Are the World." But you will hear them say, over and over, that since such a large part of our lives are now spent online, our offline selves ought to enjoy the same degree of fluidity, and that global or world citizenship isn't as much of a utopian ideal as it is a technological and historical inevitability. (Here, the techies inadvertently channel Karl Marx, who long before they were born argued that technological improvements bring about socio-economic change.)

This argument, as Harvard law professor Jack Goldsmith and Columbia law professor Tim Wu say in the 2006 book *Who Controls the Internet: Illusions of a Borderless World*, rests on faulty assumptions. Rather than indulging the Internet's laissez-faire tendencies, nation-states have not only developed the Internet but powerfully encroached upon cyberspace, using national law, technological innovations such as firewalls and filters, and financial regulation to impose border-style controls and prevent their citizens from straying too far. And they show no sign of making concessions for Bitcoin or any of the businesses it inspires; in 2013, the Federal Bureau of Investigations shut down Silk Road, an encrypted online marketplace for drugs and other contraband, that used Bitcoin and related technologies to anonymize transactions. Its founder, Ross William Ulbricht—also known as the Dread Pirate Roberts—received a life sentence in 2015 for money laundering, hacking, and conspiring to traffic narcotics.

Bitcoin's potential, Ver argues, is that since it is so heavily encrypted, there is only so much that governments can do to get in its way.

Meanwhile, his intellectual compatriots are literally trying to engineer the globe into states of their own making.

The Seasteading Institute, a nonprofit funded by PayPal co-founder Peter Thiel, promotes the creation of "seasteads," man-made autonomous islands in international waters. The islands don't actually exist—the technology isn't quite there,

and the institute is mostly run by kooky volunteers. But the
organization operates on the philosophy that the nation-state
and national citizenship should by now be obsolete, and that
people ought to "vote with their feet" and decide what kind of
government (and tax regime) they want to live under. Since the
oceans are technically international territory, little prevents
wannabe nation-builders from establishing their own territo-
ries in this no-man's land, if they can physically hack it. Patri
Friedman, the grandson of economist Milton Friedman, runs
the organization, and in doing so effectively takes the elder
Friedman's radical free-market philosophy to its logical, if
absurd, conclusion.

"There's a sense in which seasteading is an engineering
solution to the problems of politics, and that's really appealing to tech people," Friedman told me in 2012. "If we can figure
out how to build cheap modular ocean cities suddenly we solve
this huge problem in the world." Friedman referred to the business of state sovereignty as an "industry" with "a really high
barrier to entry and really high switching costs, and the cus-
tomers are getting terrible service."

Ver is a big fan of the project, and of Friedman himself,
whose political education mirrors his own. "I realized Patri is
a cool guy ten years ago," Ver said, "when I was reading his blog
and he had a picture of a bumper sticker and it said, 'Support
free trade: smuggle.'"

Ver himself started a business that helps people buy Kittitian
passports with Bitcoin. He created a website called Passports
for Bitcoin and received an enormous amount of attention
from the media, who were in equal parts outraged (you can buy

118   citizenship?) and delighted (with fake money!). It was a bust, as
the Kittitian authorities disavowed it, fearing that it would be
a security liability. When I spoke to him in February 2015, Ver
insisted that St. Kitts, or its new competitors in the citizenship
market in Antigua and beyond, will eventually come around.

"What I want to do with Passports for Bitcoin is to let other
people around the world know that if you have enough money
you can improve your situation," Ver said. "St. Kitts is here to
help you with that. I'm here to help you with that."

The Moon and Stars

On December 31, 2008, Comoro Gulf Holding rang in the new year with an open house party at the Itsandra Beach Hotel. Since Bashar Kiwan had taken over the Itsandra's management the year prior, the hotel had undergone major renovations. He had refurbished rooms and kitchens, built air-conditioned bungalows by the shore, extended the beach by several meters, and adorned the terrace with volcanic rocks to give an authentic Comorian look to the beachfront setting; he would eventually build a nightclub and install one of the country's first ATM. The operation had cost 1.2 million euros, twice the amount expected, and they still hadn't found qualified staff for some jobs locally and had to import workers from Syria. There were ongoing problems with water and electricity—problems that managers mournfully admitted they would just have to live with.

However, there was reason for hope. At a press conference held that day, Ahmad Jaroudi, the vice president of Comoro Gulf

120 Holding, repeated the company line: A new dawn was rising over the islands of the moon. Jaroudi promised that his company would make Moroni "a center that will attract the whole world, like the Palm Islands in Dubai."

"Whatever their ambitions, CGH has established a substantial, permanent presence in the Comoros, including ties to Comoran public and private elites," noted a U.S. diplomatic cable dated January 5. "While there is little tangible aside from the Itsandra Hotel, there is a lot of activity—CGH's top officials around town and on the front pages, accompanying would-be investors or signing deals. On a given day, a dozen cars with 'CGH' logos may be spotted around Moroni."

By this point, Kiwan had obtained the rights to build residential and commercial buildings on large stretches of land just outside the capital. CGH were granted customs exonerations on building equipment and a license to open a telecommunications company. The firm had plans to start an airline. That April, the Arabs even opened a private commercial bank, the Banque Federale de Commerce. Chaired by Sheikh Sabah, the bank was launched with $12 million in capital, three-quarters of it from Kiwan's own pocket, according to Africa Intelligence, a news and intelligence newsletter that covers the Indian Ocean. And the spin went on. Along the airport road, the company erected large panels advertising a development named Corniche Grande Comore. The billboards showed what seemed more like the set of a science fiction movie than feasible plans for what were essentially miles of volcanic rock, but CGH projected it would create 16,800 square meters of offices, 14,200 square meters of retail space, 7,400 square meters

of apartments, and a luxury hotel with a business center and
a marina.

The company also secured a concession from the state to build housing units around a crater lake overlooking the ocean near the northernmost tip of Moroni. Named Jannat al Kamar, or "Paradise in the Comoros," the project was described by foreign diplomats as the "crown jewel" of Comoro Gulf Holding's portfolio. Additionally, Kiwan hired SCAS Inc., a consulting firm, to draw up plans for a French call center; a greenhouse and vegetable market; a private 75-bed hospital intended to serve an "increase in tourist arrivals" and "a growing expatriate population due to the surge of business opportunities"; a prepaid electricity exchange; a cable car that would take tourists to the top of the volcano; and a dairy farm, with cows imported from Holland. The total cost of the projects would exceed $300 million, according to Africa Intelligence.

"The projects were grandiose. We couldn't pretend to do better," said former minister of foreign affairs Mohamed Sagaf. "They showed us videos of the Corniche, the port . . . it was paradise in the Comoros. And that was unimaginable, to us. But for the Arabs, it was possible. We saw what they'd achieved in Dubai, in the sea."

"All the Comorians went to the corniche to see what would soon be there. Bashar made the Comorians dream," the senior CGH manager told me. "Even I was convinced that he'd have something there someday."

Kiwan's confidence made many Comorians believe that he would be financing everything. However, CGH was not in the financial position to do so. The plan was to attract investors

122 by presenting the islands at a pair of conferences in Kuwait City and Doha in early 2010. The events were co-sponsored by the Comorian and Kuwait chambers of commerce, the United Nations Development Program, and the Arab League. Kiwan was up to his old tricks, flying Comorian delegates over in a chartered plane and putting them up in a five-star hotel, Africa Intelligence noted. The conferences took place as planned, with full presentations for each project.

Unfortunately, investors ultimately backed none of the twelve projects presented to them, and Doha was also a bust when it came to private sector pledges. According to the IMF, donors at the conference promised $540 million in aid and private Gulf investors "made sizable commitments of foreign direct investment"—but it was unclear whether the money would actually flow in, since "technical work on related projects is not completed yet, and the authorities are still uncertain about the Doha aid amounts and disbursement schedules for the coming years."

According to sources at the company, the money never came through.

"The majority of [investors] liked the Comoros, they liked the nature, but less than 1 percent wanted to invest because they saw that the environment was not conducive to business," said the senior CGH manager. "They came, they told us it was pretty, but they didn't want to pay."

The massive drop in confidence in the Gulf following Dubai's recessionary fall from grace is surely to blame for at least part of this failure. The city—as a physical place, an idea, and an investment—was looking more and more like a mirage, with photographs of abandoned luxury cars and half-built skyscrapers flooding the media. Globally, the economy was dragging as well, so it was harder to find capital for such a risky plan. Kiwan's feasibility studies insisted, pleadingly, that the Comoros were a safe bet; one claimed that because the islands produce "feel-good" commodities such as vanilla, they would "benefit overall" from the economic crisis, presumably because people eat more ice cream during a downturn. This was not a convincing sell. Repeating the great Dubai experiment in a country that could barely qualify as third-world was the last thing anyone wanted to put money on.

All of a sudden, Kiwan's heady optimism started to raise eyebrows in the land of no tomorrows. A CGH takeover didn't seem hopeful. It seemed crazy.

Here was a man who wanted to build luxury resorts on an island with virtually no running water, and who was projecting that billions could flow into the Comorian economy when gross domestic product, in current terms, the year before Sambi was inaugurated, was just $387 million. This was a country so lacking in basic infrastructure that taxi drivers went on strike for want of decent roads, hospital workers walked off the job because there weren't enough oxygen tanks, and teachers and other public servants had not been paid in months—and the man was proposing marinas, condos, and Dutch dairy cows.

"I expected nothing of him, because I saw nothing concrete," Mohamed Mchangama, the head of the Comorian consumer's union, told me in an interview in 2014. "What I saw were those posters—'Tomorrow, Dubai'—which I didn't consider at all possible."

124   Undercutting the entire project was politics. As a result of
its lobbying, in particular related to the citizenship law, CGH
was seen by more skeptical Comorians as a neo-colonizer.

       "It was the first time that a foreign private company passed
a law concerning state sovereignty. It's also the first time that a
sovereign nation gave a foreign private company the right to
profit at the expense of the state, when there were local institutions that could step in instead," wrote Houmed Msaidié in a
published debate.

       "It's been 33 years since we stopped being a French colony,"
he added. "Now we're being colonized by Comoro Gulf Holding."

Even in the absence of private investors, the citizenship
exchange with the United Arab Emirates was supposed to
generate enough windfall that it could finance infrastructure
projects and do the country some good. In the spring of 2009,
the Comorian government announced that the UAE was due
to send over $200 million in exchange for the Comoros docu-
menting 4,000 *bidoon* families of six to eight people each—
putting each citizenship at around $6,000 to $8,000. About
$25 million would go toward budgetary aid, and the remaining
$175 million would be invested in roads, sanitation, and power,
according to public statements made by President Sambi. (The
Emiratis, on their part, remained characteristically mum.)
The state, Comoro Gulf Holding, and the Combined Group, a
massive Kuwaiti contractor, would set up a joint venture to run
these works. It would be called the Comoro Combined Group,
and the state would own 33 percent, while CGH's cut was 16
percent and the Kuwaiti contractor's stake was 51 percent.

Kiwan, in other words, stood to benefit from every side of the deal.

"This will put an end to our water problems, our road problems, our energy problems," Sambi told the Comorian people on his 2009 Eid address, broadcast between sessions of the UN General Assembly in New York City and published on the Comorian presidency's website. "It will serve to build our ports, our airports, real schools to last a hundred years and the construction of a security infrastructure. My brothers, this is one of the paths I've gone down to generate wealth for our country. That's what we're missing in this country: money. And here is money, which, by the grace of God, will in the coming days be transferred into the Central Bank."

Sambi might have had God on his side, but what he really needed was someone to read him the fine print. The Ayatollah appeared to think that the money would make its way into the Comorian treasury's coffers in one piece; he failed to notice that according to Kiwan's initial contract, it was due to pass through his accounts piecemeal. Comoro Gulf Holding would presumably earn interest on the money, withhold a portion as a commission, and possibly invest it directly in the infrastructure projects to be carried out by the Combined Group. It's hard to say for sure, because the details of the deal were kept under lock and key. Kiwan did not elaborate on the deal and did not respond to repeated calls and emails after our initial November 2014 encounter.

Since 2009, international organizations have been given some clues—few of them consistent with one another—about how much money ended up in state budgets. The IMF said in 2010 that the authorities were expecting to collect 2.2 billion

Comorian francs—at the time, almost $5.3 million—in non-tax revenues from the economic citizenship program. The African Development Bank reported the following year that this represented an increase of 17.7 percent in revenues over 2009, and that the passport program was largely responsible for this growth. But the AFDB also noted, no doubt referring to contracts awarded to CGH, that "the recent trend of awarding directly negotiated concession agreements and/or barter agreements under the Law on Economic Citizenship is a major breach of the rules of economic transparency."

In 2012, at the peak of the program, the AFDB puts revenues at 5.6 percent of GDP, or $33.6 million (GDP that year was $600 million, according to the IMF). The IMF estimates the money came closer to 7.6 percent of GDP, or $45.6 million.

"The overall fiscal balance including grants improved from a deficit of 1.9 percent of GDP in 2011 to a surplus of 2.9 percent of GDP in 2012," the World Bank wrote in an annual report. "This improvement, however, was in large part explained by the growth in non-tax revenues, which came largely as a result of the revenue windfall from the Economic Citizenship Program and raised fiscal revenue from 16.1 percent in 2011 to 19.3 percent of GDP in 2012."

The following year, revenues dropped significantly, affecting the country's entire balance sheet. But record keeping in the Comoros is hardly reliable; the Interior Ministry's archives is a tiny room stacked floor to ceiling with unsorted paper. Even if the authorities were willing to divulge how much money they received and what they spent it on, there would likely be dozens of versions of the truth.

The IMF, which has tried to help Comoros reduce its crippling sovereign debt, said that even their economists were not privy to many details about the scheme. "We started to dig because we saw all this money in the budget, and we had some closed-door meetings because they were concerned about money laundering, terrorism, and what precautions were in place," said Harry Trines, who runs the Comoros desk at the IMF. He managed to set up a meeting with the authorities in 2013, but he felt that the visit had a "don't tell anybody too much" atmosphere. "We are fairly confident that money did get into the budget account, or was at least recorded as coming in," Trines said. "But what they spent it on, that I don't know."

What proportion of the cash made it into the bank is another question entirely. No one could definitively say how many passports were sold, for how much money, and how much went into Kiwan's pockets before landing in the Comoros.

Malik, the CGH manager, estimates that between 2009 and 2010—the first year of the program—the company brokered the exchange of between 5,000 and 10,000 passports, and that Kiwan received additional commissions, possibly from the Emiratis, of up to $48,000 per document, again, off the books. In an April 2015 interview, the senior CGH manager who worked closely alongside Kiwan on the ground in the Comoros put the number of passports sold during his company's heyday at between 10,000 and 15,000, at around 4,000 euros each. He said that in 2010 and 2011, he would receive calls from Kiwan once every two months to go to Sambi to fetch naturalization decrees—a list of approved names, essentially. The list, he said, was usually between 200 and 1,000 people.

128   During the last six months of Sambi's tenure, the senior manager says he personally negotiated the exchange of 10,000 passports, and that wasn't the end of it, either. "When I left, there were still suitcases of passports that were coming and going," Jaroudi said.

That puts the total somewhere around 20,000 passports over the course of two years that CGH was active in the negotiations.

Mohamed Alhadi Abbas, a former chief of staff for the Comorian interior ministry, says he believes some 60,000 passports were printed and sold to the Emirates since the program was adopted. A foreign diplomat estimates it was closer to 100,000. If these numbers are accurate, and the passports were in fact sold for the estimated $6,000 to $8,000 each, the Comorian government should have gotten at least $360 million. This would mean that hundreds of millions of dollars never saw their way into the Comorian accounts, or at least the ones that the IMF was aware of.

"I'm telling you, it's very simple," the senior manager told me. "Bashar didn't give money to the Comorians."

The Comorian government, on its part, contends that CGH did not pay out $16 million worth of funds that were supposed to go to the state. General Mohamed Dossar, who represented the state in the agreement signed in early 2008 between the Comorians, the Emiratis, and Kiwan, told me that it was "obvious that CGH did not transfer the whole amount that was owed to us" and that the contract in question was revised in late 2010.

It's undeniable that CGH gave hundreds of people jobs. But what's also clear just from looking around Moroni is that the massive infrastructure projects never saw the light of day. Anecdotally, a few roads were built; members of the diplomatic community say that some of the money went to help the government pay arrears on salaries. Besides that, very few Comorians are seeing any long-term benefit from the wholesale dissemination of their nationality. A Combined Group manager who was sent to Moroni to oversee the engineering works says his mission was aborted because the money never came through. He spent eighteen months on Grande Comore, wandering the streets at night and gazing up at the moon, which seemed close enough to touch. It was a beautiful country, he said, with the friendliest people, but the listlessness he felt led him to take up smoking again after 20 years.

"Dear Comoros Islands colleagues," he later posted on his Facebook profile. "After 18 months with Comoro Combined Group the time has come to leave and move along. I would like to thank every one of you for your support and cooperation during this period . . . and I would like to apologize to anyone [for] any misunderstanding that occurred by me."

The dream of Dubai-level development in the Indian Ocean turned out to be a sham; the Comoros gained little from the initiative. But what about the *bidoon*?

It has become clear that the bet Kiwan had made on the Gulf states providing documentation for their stateless went far beyond "economic citizenship" and papers for just 4,000 *bidoon* families in the Emirates. The entire Comorian enterprise, Kiwan's colleagues and friends say, hinged on the relocation of the *bidoon* to the Comoros, whether on their own free will or by force.

Confidential company documents support the thesis that Kiwan was banking on the mass relocation of the *bidoon* for his company's—and Comoros'—gain. In the feasibility studies commissioned by CGH, economic citizenship appears to be the foundation on which many of the large-scale developments were planned. The consultants went as far as to survey what sort of market there was for economic citizenship among the stateless; what would motivate *bidoon* families to move to the Comoros; and what kinds of profits the company could extract from their exile.

"Our recent survey in Kuwait and UAE indicates that 50% of Bidoons have been seeking a citizenship," reads one of the studies. "And when linked to real estate, 85% of the ones seeking a foreign citizenship would be interested in this value proposition."

"The crater lake and the Corniche, these were big projects to build housing for people and sell them to the governments who'd provide them, maybe for free, to [stateless] people who relocate to Comoros," says Malik. "This was the ultimate plan."

The senior CGH manager who spoke on condition of anonymity said that Kiwan rationalized his endeavor by saying that the *bidoon* would be more likely to become Emirati if they became Comorian first. "This could be a beneficial arrangement for the Comorians and the *bidoon*," he said. "But I think Bashar wanted above all to make money. He's very diplomatic, so he'd never say it, and he passed himself off as benevolent, but I personally think he couldn't have cared less about the *bidoon* or the Comorians."

If the Gulf governments were, in fact, committed to solving their *bidoon* problem by exporting the stateless population, as Kiwan seemed to believe they would; if they had money to spend on this venture, and the brute power to make it happen against their peoples' will, or if the *bidoon* would, in fact, become Comorians in both name and residence, possibly even buying their own properties; then there would be an enormous market for housing, services, telecommunications, and even dairy cows. The presence of the *bidoon* would help native Comorians, who would benefit from increased investment in their country. It would bring in outside business to cater to the *bidoon's* needs. The government would get the one thing it needed the most: money. And the newly Comorian *bidoon* would finally have a place to call home.

St. Kitts was doing it. Dominica was doing it. Austria did it. Even Canada had done it, in its own way. Why not take the concept one step further?

"None of us thought of the effects of economic citizenship. We believed in the project and didn't take anything else into consideration—we weren't thinking about the hidden intentions," says Malik. "We were living the project, seeing Corniche billboards, crater lake billboards, investments in telecom, mini ports . . . see[ing] that happening in a country like that and [being] involved in everything and controlling everything gave me a high sense of achievement and satisfaction which I haven't found anywhere else."

Elie Wakim, a close friend and associate of Kiwan's who says he helped pitch the Comoros proposal to the Emirati government in a closed-door meeting, came to embrace the initiative. "I understand very well that people might be shocked by this principle," he said over Skype. "But these are people who have no country, who are spread out over the Arab world, who can't travel or have an identity or hold certain jobs without facing discrimination."

"It's an idea that's developing, and there are societies that can help," he added, citing, as an example, "I can have a St. Kitts passport without having any attachment."

Kiwan, meanwhile, was turning his attention on Kuwait, hoping to land the next big deal, his friends and associates say. The Emirati *bidoon* were in the bag, but during the Comorians' 2008 visit, the Kuwaiti government had all but stonewalled the delegation, and there had been little progress since.

A business acquaintance of Kiwan's in Kuwait says that Kiwan asked him in 2009 to speak to Mussalam al-Barrak, the country's garrulous opposition leader, and talk (or bribe) him into accepting the Comoros solution. "Bashar talked about the pressure that the Abu Dhabi government put on the *bidoon* to accept the deal, forcing them to have no choice but to take Comoros citizenship," he said.

"'What will the *bidoon* care about the situation?' [Bashar] asked me. 'It's not like they will lose anything. They won't have to pay even a single Dinar. The government will pay for all of it.'"

Kiwan's efforts went nowhere at the time. Human rights activists speculate the proposal fell through because the opposition and the *bidoon* rights movement were gaining momentum; Kiwan says the Emirates wanted exclusivity on the program; Comorian officials say Kuwait backed out because the two countries could not agree on terms.

Besides, Kiwan's luck in Moroni was beginning to run dry. In order to secure a telecom license to operate Twama Telecom in 2007, Comoro Gulf Holding had promised to build a small port as collateral. But the company never followed through on the construction, which grew into a serious point of contention with government officials and the population at large.

CGH lost its telecom license, which led to a lawsuit from an Emirati prince and tycoon, Talal al Khoury. Khoury—who's best known for spending $9 million on a UAE license plate sporting only the number "5" —had invested $17 million in the company in 2007, when the future looked bright. But when he came to the islands some years later and realized the Comorian company he thought he owned three-quarters of did not, in fact, exist, he demanded that Kiwan repay him, according to Khoury's lawyer, Ibrahim Ali Mzimba.

An Abu Dhabi judge ruled that Kiwan had not breached any agreements, because Khoury did not pay the full sum that he'd promised as part of his initial investment, Mzimba told me. The case was then heard in Moroni, where Khoury's legal team was given the go-ahead to seize some of Bashar's local business assets to repay the prince. But Mzimba says that anything of value was off-limits thanks to complex corporate ownership structures that made it seem like Kiwan didn't own anything.

It turned out that the pitfalls of doing business in Comoros in 2011 were the same as the ones Bob Denard encountered in the eighties: Everything, at some point, gets personal on a tiny, secluded island. And with President Sambi's term due to end that year, the concessions that Kiwan had obtained could evaporate overnight. It didn't help that Sambi and Kiwan had something of a falling out in the final months of the presidency. The business of the unfinished ports had made Sambi look naïve,

134   even downright stupid, for putting his unwavering faith in the company for so long. He began to give Bashar the cold shoulder. Then, the men got into a bizarre public spat over Comoros' support for the Libyan leader Muammar Gaddafi. In Comoros, Gaddafi is remembered fondly as a freedom fighter and a profligate donor; over the course of Gaddafi's rule, Libya contributed security, boats, and building materials to the islands in aid. In 2008, Libya donated 700,000 euros directly to the islands (the U.S. contributed just a half million) and the following year, the country built a school block. But Kiwan was apparently no fan of the dictator, and believed the Comoros should stop praising him publicly when the international community was out for his head.

On March 14, 2011, an editorial accusing the Sambi regime of "a regrettable error of judgment that could lead to incalculable consequences for the Comoros"—referring to its public support of Gaddafi—appeared in the CGH-owned newspaper *Al-Balad*. The Gaddafi issue was symbolic of a bigger problem: Kiwan was overstepping as a businessman. *Al-Balad* had already found itself embroiled in inter-island politics when Kiwan began publishing a version of the paper in the island of Mayotte the year prior. Mayotte belongs to France but is considered by the other three islands as rightfully Comorian; creating a separate publication for the island was tantamount to treason.

That May, a politician named Ikililou Dhoinine who'd served as one of Sambi's vice presidents was sworn into office as the new president after winning 61 percent of the vote. His term signaled the beginning of the end for the Arabs. The new administration began to pressure the company to pay back the missing $16 million it had apparently withheld from the economic citizenship program, and revoked the privileged status that Sambi had afforded Kiwan during his tenure.

Still, the passport money kept coming. Ikililou's cabinet put in place some reforms to the program—most significantly that the money from the Emirates be paid directly to the Comorian government rather than passing through intermediary accounts—but this did little to quell suspicion over where the funds were ultimately kept. Ikililou also put in place a commission to review each citizenship application, as the initial law had mandated, but even members of the commission told me they thought the due diligence was weak; according to sources in the Comoros, the Emirati ministry of the interior handled the processing and the bulk of the vetting of applications before sending the applicants' personal information to the Comoros for final review. Once the commission was done, the Ministry of the Interior would see to it that the passports were printed, cram them in a suitcase, and send a representative to the UAE to hand the suitcase full of passports to the Emiratis.

It was only a matter of time until these suitcases became the subject of a scandal. In the summer of 2013, Abou Achirafi, the head of the Comorian national security agency, was discovered to have been engaging in a passport-selling hustle of his own. He ran his operation under the nose of the local Interpol office, with which his department shares a compound, and was arrested at the Comoros airport with a suitcase full of passports.

By that time, Kiwan had been all but driven out of the Comoros, and his businesses were suffering. The Itsandra, for all its glitz and glamor, was apparently low on clients. "Diplomats and members of foreign missions who visit Moroni and stay at the Hotel Itsandra are privately surprised by the very low rate of occupancy of the rooms and bungalows," reported Africa Intelligence. French authorities were reportedly giving the Banque Fédérale de Commerce a hard time over money-laundering compliance, which slowed operations considerably. (The bank has never formally been accused of illicit activity.) In early 2014, Kiwan lost his lease on the Itsandra and his concessions at the Corniche and around the crater lake. And that July, the Corniche placards were torn down.

"The destruction of this long barrier of panels, which at one point, captured the popular imagination . . . marks the end of an era that led people to believe, as Bashar Kiwan had promised them, that a paradise village would bloom from this site," a local blogger wrote.

In May 2015, Moroni's high court ruled that Comoro Gulf Holding owed 8 billion Comorian francs—or the missing $16 million—from the economic citizenship program to the state, and allowed the seizure of company assets on the islands—184 pieces of machinery, a stockroom, and three large piles of sand at the company's cement facility, according to Al-Watwan—to move forward. According to the paper, the BFC took over some of these assets in August 2012, perhaps to protect them from seizure (on paper, the BFC is unaffiliated with Comoro Gulf Holding, according to the senior manager).

"What preoccupies me are the socio-economic implications of this affair," Elie Yasbech, the company representative on the ground, told the paper. "I'm defending a humanitarian cause; I'm on the side of the employees who will soon be out of work."

Bashar's paper, *Al-Balad*, had never turned a profit, either; it was being given out for free ten months after its launch, and folded after serving as a Kiwan mouthpiece for two years.

In December 2014, piles of back issues lay strewn among long-abandoned printing equipment in a large shed adjacent to the newspaper's old offices on a quiet side street near Moroni. In one of the final issues, a regular sidebar about "French wisdom" explained the meaning of an idiom.

"*Il ne faut pas croire qui promet la lune,*" it reads. "One should not believe he who promises the moon and stars."

Native Sons

Ahmed Abdul Khaleq landed in Bangkok on July 16, 2012, a Thai visitor visa attached to his Comorian passport. When he stepped up to the customs desk, a puzzled immigration officer asked him where his passport was from.

"It's from the Comoros," Khaleq said. "It's in Africa."

"So you're African?" the officer said. "But you're white!"

"Yes," Khaleq sighed. "I'm a white African."

He was met at the exit by a representative from the UN's Office of the High Commissioner for Human Rights, who held up a big sign with his name on it. In a hotel room paid for by the UN, Khaleq slept that night quite legally for the first time in his life.

He woke up the next morning and couldn't entirely believe where he was. Activists had been skeptical that the UAE would even follow through on their deportation threats in the first place because the move seemed so extreme. "I hope that UAE authorities are just trying to mess with him and the deportation wouldn't go through since they would get a lot of horrible press about this," one Human Rights Watch officer wrote in an internal email a week earlier. "It would set a horrible precedent." When the organization realized Khaleq was, in fact, on his way to Thailand, they rushed out a press release denouncing the Gulf country's actions. "UAE authorities are trying to make it appear as though Ahmed Abd al-Khaleq is choosing to leave the country on his own volition, but this is a cruel and unlawful expulsion by duress, plain and simple," said Sarah Leah Whitson, the organization's Middle East director, in the statement. "The UAE authorities are ever creative in coming up with outrageous tactics to silence dissenting voices."

Under ordinary circumstances, it can take months, years, or even decades for refugees to obtain the necessary approvals to start new lives elsewhere. But Khaleq's case was fast-tracked— in part to deter the Emirate authorities from repeating the process with another unsuspecting *bidoon*, but also because it was unclear how long the Thai authorities would tolerate Khaleq's presence in Bangkok. Thaksin Shinawatra, the former Thai prime minister (and erstwhile "economic" Montenegrin), was close with the UAE authorities, and retained a lot of clout. Advocates worried that Khaleq's life would become more difficult if he continued his rabble-rousing, and Thaksin's friends in Dubai pushed for his expulsion. Khaleq had spoken to Reuters and the *Bangkok Post* about his predicament when he arrived, and the next day he was advised to stop doing interviews. He mostly kept offline and wore hats in public to maintain anonymity. He even bought a crowbar, which he still keeps in his closet in Ontario, to protect himself should someone come for him at night.

140   After spending a night in the hotel, Khaleq moved into an apartment, where he stayed for almost two months. A neighbor, it turns out, was legitimately from the Comoros. They would run into each other in the lobby and talk about their shared country. "I said, you are the original, I am the duplicate." He spoke to his family on Skype and felt another new emotion: homesickness.

Over the summer, Khaleq obtained his asylum approval and was assigned to emigrate to London, Ontario, a Canadian city not far from Detroit. On September 11, he flew to Toronto via Hong Kong, then boarded a bus that took him to London. The Cross Cultural Learner Centre a non-profit that helps refugees integrate into their new communities, helped him find an apartment, sign up for English lessons, and get his precious library card.

Today, Khaleq is training to become a manager of a Pizza Pizza franchise he bought, after selling a convenience store he ran at a profit. He'll soon become eligible for Canadian citizenship, and hopes he'll be rid of his Comorian passport, too. He and his roommate—a Kurdish refugee who recently moved from Russia—joke that when they obtain their papers, they'll go back to Thailand, but this time on vacation.

Meanwhile, the Comorians continued to issue passports to the Emirati *bidoon*. Kiwan was long gone by the time Khaleq was on his grand tour, but the program he'd helped set up was still going strong, and revenues from passport money in 2012 were believed to be at their highest. The *bidoon* were told that taking Comorian economic citizenship was the first step to becoming Emirati, so many signed up willingly, flocking to the squat building to which Khaleq had initially been summoned before his imprisonment and exile. There, Emirati officials signed up hundreds of *bidoon* families for foreign citizenship as though they were receiving food stamps or driver's licenses.

Local news reports in the Emirates indicated that thousands had been documented in *bidoon* neighborhoods. In July 2008, the Gulf News agency reported that the Emirati interior minister, Saif bin Zayed Al Nahyan, had "recommended" twenty-five Interior Ministry employees for UAE citizenship after they'd obtained Comorian passports. His right-hand man, Nasser Salem Saif Lekhreiban Al Nuaimi—with whom Kiwan and the Comorians signed their 2008 agreement—made the announcement. It is unclear if these stateless people actually ended up becoming naturalized; Al Nuaimi did not respond to interview requests, and little has been revealed about the outcome of the plan since it began.

It is also unclear whether the passports will be renewed by the Comorian government when they expire—if not, the Comorian *bidoon* will become stateless once more. Either way, the *bidoon* continue to live as second-class residents.

The passports, meanwhile, give the Emirati state an opportunity to further stratify their society, and hold the *bidoon* apart from the native population both in practice and on paper. To this day, there are almost weekly reports in the Abu Dhabi press of rapes, murders, assaults, and robberies committed in the Emirates by Comorian passport-holders.

The public naming and shaming of these "Comorian" criminals has proven to be a considerable inconvenience for ordinary, native Comorians: Some countries began to require all Comorians to obtain visas before traveling—even former heads of state. "To travel to a place like Egypt, we used to just get visas at the airport," said ex-president Azali. "Today we have to obtain one in advance. Egypt is suspicious of Comorians. And that's one of the first notable consequences of this program, since we can't move around as freely as we could before."

On a Sunday evening in November 2014, Hakeem al-Fadhli, Kuwait's most militant *bidoon* activist, was finishing a dinner of shrimp, salad, hummus, and freshly baked bread at an out-door Persian restaurant in the Souk al Mubarakiya, a market in Kuwait City. It was a warm night with almost no humidity, and a musky scent embalmed the air each time a group of men dressed in robes and doused in *oud* walked by. The market is al-Fadhli's favorite spot in Kuwait; in a city that has been overtaken by oil-industry money, its fruit stands and bustling aisles have a rare *gemütlich* feel.

The 39-year-old al-Fadhli became an activist in early 2011 when he attended a *bidoon* rights rally and became radicalized when he saw the police dragging away his brother and friends for simply demanding citizenship rights. The story he tells is typical: His family had been living on Kuwaiti soil for genera-tions and yet could not obtain citizenship because al-Fadhli's grandfather, an oil worker, had failed to register with the right authorities at the right time. They had been treated with sus-picion after the Iraqi invasion, denied access to education and healthcare, and accused of being from Iraq—and therefore, an enemy of the state.

Al-Fahdli started to organize rallies and went door to door persuading young *bidoon* to support his cause. He eventually quit his job as an auto engineer to commit to his cause full-time, and he spent months behind bars. When I met him in Kuwait City in 2014, al-Fadhli was still recovering his strength after a hunger strike he'd participated in to protest the conditions of his detention. After his big dinner, al-Fadhli ordered strong black tea, which came in small shot-sized glasses filled halfway with white sugar. He stirred his cup, and was about to take a sip when his phone began vibrating and a news story popped up on the screen. BIDOON TO COMOROS, the headline to the story read.

Mazen al-Jarrah, a Kuwaiti Interior Ministry official, had announced that the government would arrange for the Kuwaiti *bidoon* to register for Comorian citizenship in exchange for aid. But the Comorians would also be on the hook to accept any deported *bidoon* if the Kuwaiti government decided they didn't want them around anymore. The *bidoon* would not have to pay a dime, and the application process would begin in about a month's time.

Al-Fadhli was livid. All the *bidoon* knew about Khaleq's deportation. Mona Kareem, a Kuwaiti *bidoon* blogger, told al-Fadhli in a message that she felt her heart was going to explode. "I went to bed West Asian & woke up East African," she posted on Twitter. Just days earlier, the United Nations High Commissioner for Refugees had launched a campaign to end statelessness; it was hard to imagine that the bulk sale of Comorian passports was the response they'd hoped for.

"The Kuwaiti government is engaging in apartheid against the *bidoon*," al-Fadhli told me. "We will not allow them to sell us to the Comoros. This is a human trafficking crime."

144   He surmised that those who are outspoken will be deported. "I will definitely be the first."

A few days later, I met Mazen al-Jarrah at his office in the Kuwaiti Interior Ministry. A handsome middle-aged man wearing an impressive gray slug of a mustache and a heavily decorated police uniform, al-Jarrah belonged to Kuwait's ruling Sabah family. In a matter-of-fact way, he informed me that the *bidoon* would be given bona fide Comorian citizenship, with no bars on living on the islands, and that the status would come with a five-year residence visa that would allow them to stay in Kuwait. Mass expulsions were not planned, but "those that do commit crimes will be sent to the Comoros Islands [*sic*] where they will be provided with a private apartment in the buildings that Kuwait invested in," he said.

The plan was based on the Emirati program, he said, but it was very important for Kuwait to have the option of sending criminals to the islands, with the archipelago serving the Kuwaitis as a kind of penal colony. Hearing al-Jarrah speak, it is difficult not to recall the Nazis' plan to delay exterminating Polish Jews and ship them off to Madagascar instead. Franz Rademacher, the mastermind behind the so-called Madagascar plan, even suggested that the forced deportations would show how benevolent the German people were toward their undesirable compatriots—a sentiment al-Jarrah echoed when listing the many benefits the Kuwaitis would provide for their exiles from afar.

Life in the Comoros was a perfectly reasonable demand, al-Jarrah seemed to think, since only a fraction of the *bidoon* would suffer this fate; the rest of the Comorian *bidoon* would be welcome to stay and work in Kuwait. (Never mind that a few months later, dozens of *bidoon* were fired from their temporary government jobs for no apparent reason.)

Al-Jarrah, who had attained the rank of major general, planned to start by documenting the *bidoon* in the army. "There are around 1,000 stateless in the army and police that will be the first to be forced to either take Comoros citizenship or leave the country," he explained. "These 1,000 represent families as well, of course, so around 10,000 people." He made it clear that the *bidoon* would not have a choice in the matter.

Al-Jarrah insisted that the *bidoon* were given the same opportunities and were as prosperous as ordinary Kuwaitis. This is patently not the case: a walk through the *bidoon* neighborhood of Taima, with its cinder-block houses and gravel roads, is a depressing sight, and on a recent visit parents complained that they weren't able to sign up their children to go to school. Al-Jarrah then picked up his phone and texted me a picture of a *bidoon* soccer star posing next to two fancy cars. The player was a young man named Fahad al Enezi, and he was the talk of the town: The night before, al Enezi had scored the winning goal in a Gulf Cup match against Iraq.

The irony of a stateless man deprived of Kuwaiti citizenship winning a soccer game for the Kuwaiti national team against the country's historical enemy—an enemy that the *bidoon* were once accused of collaborating with—seemed completely lost on the minister.

After he'd finished explaining how good the *bidoon* have it, and how proud he was of the Comoros initiative, I asked al-Jarrah why it was permissible to sell Comorian but not Kuwaiti citizenship. He looked at me like I'd asked him an unforgivably stupid question.

"Our citizenship is expensive!" he said. "Here we take care of every citizen's needs from when he is born until he dies. All of his expenses: healthcare, school, everything. Do you know what the benefits of our citizenship are? They pay for our marriages, give us work, pay for our housing, our retirement," he said.

So what does it mean to him to be a citizen of Kuwait? I asked.

"What can I say, other than that it is great?"

Since al-Jarrah and I spoke, very little has been revealed about the Comoros-Kuwait scheme he'd announced, or how much money the islands are still receiving from their first foray into selling passports. The IMF in 2013 reported that the citizenship program had been shut down, but a year later, its representative said money was still trickling in, albeit in tiny amounts. After its last review in early 2015, the IMF noted that Comorian authorities "indicated that they were optimistic that a new ECP program with Kuwait would be agreed," and added that the agency "urged the introduction of strong safeguards to prevent the misuse of the program for illegitimate purposes and to ensure its sustainability."

But diplomats on the ground say that the two countries can't agree on whether forced deportations will figure into the deal.

Bashar Kiwan, for his part, claimed no knowledge of the affair and denied having any involvement in it at all. When I met him in his office just minutes away from the Interior Ministry in Kuwait's city center, he claimed to have heard the news the same way I did—from the papers. His relationship with the Comorian government was still bad, and he claimed Comoro Gulf Holding had lost a lot of money. Kiwan believed he was being poorly treated given that he invested so much time and money into what he described as an essentially humanitarian effort to help the country get back on its feet.

He also appeared to have changed his mind about the Kuwaiti *bidoon*—perhaps now that he could no longer make money off of them. He told me that they should not be given Comorian passports or sent away to the islands. "I think that a large number of the *bidoon* deserve Kuwaiti citizenship," he said.

Before leaving, I asked Kiwan what citizenship meant to him, as a Franco-Syrian with diplomatic Comorian credentials and businesses all over the world. What were his rights, duties, and obligations? Where did he belong?

"I'm a Syrian who's always lived outside my country," he replied.

"So for me, citizenship doesn't mean much."

The following week, I visited Kiwan's villa in the Comoros. Nestled in an overgrowth of pineapple trees and palms, the place was abandoned and boarded up. Goats grazed at the entrance to the estate; the pool, which overlooked the brilliant blue ocean, ran dry, and his guesthouse stood empty. An emaciated, elderly watchman, who said he was still being paid by Kiwan to guard the place, told me the house was mostly used as a love den by parliamentarians cheating on their wives.

Then, I returned to the corniche, where Kiwan's giddy vision was once displayed for the island to see. There was nothing left of it except reams of multi-colored trash creeping into the ocean and extending as far as the eye could see up the coastline. The only trace of Comoro Gulf Holding was a partially constructed building with the blue and white CGH logo, once ubiquitous in Moroni, now bleached out and fading in the sun. Locals observed that with the disappearance of the panels, taxi drivers had lost their mile-long toilet.

Another man stood by the building, guarding the premises. He led me to a shed, where he unlocked a rolldown gate to reveal a CGH-branded gas pump—a remnant of the hopes that once seized the archipelago, then floated away.

Kiwan was still paying his salary, too, he said. He hadn't seen the boss in a while. But he hoped and dreamed that he would return.

Things were better, he said, when Bashar Kiwan was around.

Afterword

The *bidoon* have been the focus of this book, but they are not the only stateless people living in the world today. The Muslim Rohingya in Buddhist Myanmar are ceaselessly persecuted and denied citizenship rights because of their religion. A 2014 court ruling in the Dominican Republic rendered thousands of citizens of Haitian origin stateless overnight, then called for their deportation "back" to Haiti, even if they'd never set foot in "their" country before. These cases illustrate that the only thing worse than being a second-class citizen is being a second-class non-citizen.

The discriminatory policies and limits on human mobility that create these problems are political to their core, and you don't even have to be stateless for them to affect you. Take last summer's crisis at the U.S. border, during which droves of unaccompanied children from South America turned up seeking sanctuary. Or consider the deaths of thousands of refugees who crossed the Mediterranean by boat to escape violence in North

152   Africa, and the lack of empathy on the part of the European governments who stand to receive them.

Our citizenship still determines who can go where, when,
how, and for how long; even in times when citizenship can
be bought, sold, renounced, and revoked; even at a moment
when there are more refugees displaced from their homes than
there have been since World War II; even when cross-border trade
and technology have diluted the ties between citizens, strength-
ened bonds between geographical strangers, and revealed a fresh
layer of arbitrariness to our national allegiances.

The most fundamental reasons for these crises are the per-
sistent impenetrability of national borders, the limits on the free
movement of people, and the lack of political will to ease them.
As we've seen, everyone—even the 0.01 percent—is affected.
But it's hard not to notice that the "quality," so to speak, of citizenships and visa restrictions falls largely along economic and
ethnic lines. The sinking ships move from East to West. The
migrants move from South to North. Along these journeys, a
hierarchy of passports emerges: German, good. Swedish, good.
Canadian, good. Afghan, bad. This taxonomy has its own terms of
art: Wealthy and white, you're an expat; hard-working and from a
third-world country, you're an immigrant; poor or black or on the
brink of death, you're a migrant.

Commenting on French TV about the plight of migrants
drowning in the Atlantic on the way to Fortress Europe, the
Senegalese novelist Fatou Diome remarked:

You see on the headline the flow of African migrants arriving in Europe but you don't speak of the Europeans going

in Africa. That's the free flow of the powerful, the ones who
have the money, and the right kind of passports. You go
to Senegal, to Mali, to any country around the world. . . .
Anywhere I go, I meet French people, Germans, and Dutch.
I see them everywhere around the world, because they have
the right passport. With your passport, you go anywhere
around the world, and act like you run those place, with
your pretentious demeanor. Stop the hypocrisy. We will all
be rich together, or perish together.

A Liberian academic, writing for the blog Africa Is a Country,
recounted her experience of being denied a seat on an Emirates
flight to Dubai because the UAE, concerned about the spread
of infectious disease, had barred anyone with a Liberian passport from so much as visiting. "This was punishment for simply being born in Africa with a particular African passport,"
she wrote:

Never mind that Liberia was declared Ebola-free exactly one
month ago. Never mind that I have not been to my homeland
in over 10 months. I've seen my passport scrutinized more
intently than ever before. . . . If I were traveling directly from
Guinea, Liberia, or Sierra Leone and had a passport from
a country on UAE's list of exemptions, I would have gotten a
visa on arrival with ease. No questions asked.

The story of citizenship in the twenty-first century is thus at
its core another example of the stark inequality between the

154   West and the South, the rich and the poor. Not all passports
        were created equal; not all nationalities are considered equally
        desirable. The very same countries who reject the poor arriv-
        ing by sea roll out the red carpet for wealthy investors who
        can pay for papers. In a world where all humans are theoreti-
        cally born equal, the fact remains that some people have ten
        passports, while others have none—again, largely as a result
        of state-sanctioned discrimination. (Arendt's line about the
        "right to have rights" seems more relevant than ever.)

        In this context, the sale of citizenship is interesting
        not because it is scandalous or even morally reprehensible,
        but because it speaks to the very arbitrariness of the concept
        of belonging to a nation to begin with. In 2002, the political
        scientist Samuel Huntington—the man credited with coin-
        ing the term "Davos Man" to describe the type of global elite
        who attend the annual World Economic Forum in the Swiss
        city—published an essay on the rift between the wealthi-
        est Americans and the rest of the country in the conservative
        international affairs magazine *The National Interest*. The elites,
        Huntington writes in "Dead Souls: The Denationalization
        of the American Elite," are seceding into global units of one,
        while the public is growing more skeptical of globalization
        and becoming increasingly patriotic. (It's worth noting that
        he was writing in the direct aftermath of the September 11
        attacks.) "Nationalism has proven wrong Karl Marx's con-
        cept of a unified international proletariat," Huntington wrote.
        "Globalization is proving right Adam Smith's observation that
        while 'the proprietor of land is necessarily a citizen of the par-
        ticular country in which his estate lies . . . the proprietor of

stock is properly a citizen of the world, and is not necessarily attached to any particular country.'"

Roger Ver, Patri Friedman, and Eduardo Saverin have this in common: They chose to opt out.

The "financialization" of citizenship isn't just a problem for traditionalists like Huntington. It's also a disturbing trend for supporters of participatory democracy, social welfare programs, and wealth redistribution. Peter Spiro, a legal scholar at Temple University and the author of several books on citizenship law, situates the breakdown of national citizenship in a broader context of mounting income and wealth inequality within nations. (Spiro, alongside philosopher Martha Nussbaum and former UN Secretary General Kofi Annan, is named by Huntington as an example of "transnational" intellectuals who "abandon their commitment to their nation and their fellow citizens and argue the moral superiority of identifying with humanity at large.") Citing Thomas Piketty's best-selling *Capital in the Twenty-First Century*, Spiro summed up the book to a glassy-eyed crowd at a Henley & Partners conference in 2014 at which he was invited to speak: "The take away line was that inequality was suppressed during the twentieth century. The reason for that was that that was a period of great conflict along state lines, individuals felt like they could share with their fellow citizens." These days, Spiro went on to argue, people just do not share in quite the same way, because the social meanings attached to citizenship have broken down. That's why practices like tax avoidance are expected and even permissible, and why so many countries now allow dual citizenship—a status that Teddy Roosevelt once likened to polygamy.

Ultimately, it is this disconnect between the place and the person, the citizen and the community, that allowed the Emirates to buy citizenship for the *bidoon*, and why the Comorians allowed themselves to sell it. "To the extent that the social membership part of the equation has been taken out, it becomes a commodity that's now increasingly going to be governed by market parameters," Spiro said.

But if the whole premise of national citizenship was built on the common cause of the nation, and if the nation is being called into question as a result of globalizing technology, trade, and crisis, it makes perfect sense for our connection and allegiance to the nation to be challenged too. In retrospect, it seems crazy to think that an institution like national citizenship could remain unaffected by globalization.

Which brings us to "global" citizenship. "Global" or "world citizenship" was not always a cynical enterprise dead-set on extracting value from impoverished former colonies that have nothing else to sell. It did not aspire to help the so-called 1 percent live borderless lives while making actual stateless people the unwitting victims of its traffic. The terms have long since served as a catchphrase, of course—sprinkled liberally in the names of progressive schools and do-gooder nonprofits and even creeping their way into copy for corporate social-responsibility websites. But years before Jay-Z and Kanye West rapped about avoiding incarceration with five passports, John Lennon imagined a world with no war, no borders, no countries, and, presumably, no rivaling nationalities or visa restrictions on the movement of Russian and Chinese citizens. Millennia before the formerly French actor Gerard Depardieu told the press he'd renounced his citizenship not to avoid taxes but because he was a citizen of the world, Diogenes declared that he was not a mere citizen of Athens, but a citizen of the world too.

Today, much of this idealism has been stripped away. "Global citizenship can be used and abused in contexts that have nothing to do with citizenship," sighed Roehampton professor Darren O'Byrne when I asked him what had become of the concept. "It's becoming a postmodern free-floating signifier unattached to any meaning. It becomes emptied of the concepts that Garry Davis struggled to push. And this corporate hijacking of the term is a very real danger."

Then again, there have always been competing versions of the cosmopolitan ethos. For every Cynic who dreams of personal secession, there will be a starry-eyed Stoic trying to hug the entirety of humanity; for ever Garry Davis, there will be a Roger Ver. The vision that prevails will be tremendously consequential. National citizenship, while by no means irrelevant on a practical level, is beginning to show its cracks as an institution. Countries are themselves undermining the very imaginings on which they were built, most explicitly by endorsing the sale of citizenship for short-term profit.

If the nation-state is, in fact, losing relevance, ought we all aspire to be more global, and risk becoming unmoored and uprooted in the process? Can we truly divorce ourselves from geography and territory? Will technologies such as Bitcoin offer their own imaginings, changing the way we think about our communities and each other?

From a policy standpoint: can sovereign nations adapt their version of what it means to be a citizen into something more relevant to the way we live now, or ought they try to shore up the twentieth-century nationalism that proved successful in both redistributing resources and starting wars? Will countries keep competing to host the best, brightest, and richest "global citizens" by coaxing them over with tax breaks and passports, or will they start paying attention to those who need help in their own back yards? Will borders open up and let more people through, or will states close their doors and admit only a select few based on their wealth, status, and qualifications?

These questions might sound abstract, but they're playing out before our eyes every day. When Scotland voted on whether to secede from the U.K. in 2014, the "yes" camp presented a softer, more inclusive, more progressive vision of what it means to be Scottish, pledging support both to the country's social safety net and to more open immigration. The U.K., on the other hand, requires foreigners to make a minimum salary in order to live and work within its borders, and political parties across Europe (and beyond) employ increasingly xenophobic, anti-immigrant rhetoric, most likely in reaction to economic hardship, but also from a place of deep-rooted racism.

Estonia has come up with another model: electronic citizenship. Anyone in the world can sign up to use the country's online infrastructure to open a business or register a domain name, and the state expects ten million new "E-stonians" by 2025. Their approach is inclusive and completely decentralized—anybody can register, and a visit to Tallinn is optional. But e-citizenship remains a fundamentally commercial initiative, and one that reveals how acutely transactional the notion of belonging has become. It overwhelmingly and unsurprisingly

benefits the rich: Geography, ethnicity, and religion matter less
than wealth, Internet access, and business savvy.

This "corporate hijacking" of citizenship may be ubiquitous. The idea that the citizen is, above all, a consumer, is taking
hold worldwide. But that doesn't make it a sustainable vision.
Much bigger problems loom ahead.

Over the next few decades, entire nations will likely be sub-
merged by rising seawater. The need for binding international
cooperation to curb climate change is critical, but on the ground,
the question is existential. Where will Maldivians be "from" if
they lose the ground beneath their feet? Will a new Nansen step
in and create passports for climate refugees? Or will those displaced by the deluge end up bidding for a new nationality on the
open market?

These are the stakes of citizenship in the twenty-first
century.

Benedict Anderson, *Imagined Communities: Reflections on the Origin and Spread of Nationalism* (Verso, 1983). Benedict Anderson's *Imagined Communities* is widely regarded as the most important book in print on the origins of nationalism—and, by extension, nationality. The book draws from history, literature, politics, and theory to document how individuals living in a country came to consider each other compatriots. It's worth reading and re-reading; it's also wonderfully written.

Edward Everett Hale, "The Man Without a Country," *The Atlantic Monthly*, December 1863 (http://www.theatlantic.com/magazine/archive/1863/12/the-man-without-a-country/308751/). On May 19, 1863, Abraham Lincoln expelled an Ohio congressman named Clement Vallandigham from the Union for speaking out against the war and expressing sympathy for the Confederate cause. Edward Everett Hale, a writer and Unitarian minister, was so outraged by Vallandigham's statements that he wrote "The Man Without a Country," a cautionary tale inspired by the events intended to discourage Americans from behaving unpatriotically. The story tells the tale of a treasonous protagonist, Philip Nolan, who is sent off to sea for criticizing the Union; it's been adapted for film and radio multiple times. But little could Hale have known that, a century and a half later, American citizens would choose exile of their own volition.

Ayelet Shachar, *The Birthright Lottery: Citizenship and Global Inequality* (Harvard University Press, 2009). Citizenship is inherited by blind luck and plays a tremendous role in determining our fates. Given that it is so unfairly and arbitrarily assigned, shouldn't there be a way to redistribute its benefits in a just society? *The Birthright Lottery* frames the acquisition of citizenship as a problem of distribution, not unlike the inheritance of wealth, and discusses the responsibilities of citizens in wealthy nations to help their less fortunate peers.

Peter Spiro, *Beyond Citizenship: American Identity After Globalization* (Oxford, 2008) and *At Home in Two Countries: The Past and Future of Dual Citizenship* (NYU, 2016). Because Peter Spiro writes regularly on citizenship in a post-national context, he's frequently invited by leaders in the passport industry to speak at events. He's also one of the first scholars I spoke to about the business of selling citizenship, back in 2011. In *Beyond Citizenship*, Spiro's main thesis is that twentieth-century ideas about American citizenship don't hold up anymore, and that bonds between Americans, which once largely rested on their common American-ness, are being replaced by other commonalities: politics, sexuality, gender, shared interests, race, and business. His most recent

book, *At Home in Two Countries*, explains how dual citizenship has gone from
being regarded as a threat to international society, to an almost prosaic status
held by diasporas, business elites, and people of mixed heritage.

Joseph O'Neill, *The Dog: A Novel* (Random House, 2014). *The Dog* came out
as I was reporting the stories that ultimately ended up in this book. Reading
it was downright eerie, because it is, thematically at least, *The Cosmopolites'*
fictional equivalent. Set in pre-recessionary Dubai with a jet-set, rootless
lawyer as the main protagonist, O'Neill conveys a deep-rooted anxiety about
what it means to be an ethical person on a global scale. The book even features
a stateless servant who acquires Comorian citizenship and is sent away from
the Emirates.

Patrick Weil, *The Sovereign Citizen: Denaturalization and the Origins of the
American Republic* (University of Pennsylvania Press, 2012). The best-known
cases of denationalization occurred in Nazi Germany, but until the 1970s,
the United States would routinely strip Americans of their citizenship for
political and administrative reasons. Patrick Weil, a visiting law professor
at Yale and a research fellow at the French National Centre for Scientific
Research, pored over Supreme Court archives to write a meticulous history of
denationalization law in the United States, from the deportation of anarchist
Emma Goldman to *Afroyim v. Rusk*, the ruling establishing that U.S. citizenship
cannot be involuntarily taken away from a citizen by the state. This history
is particularly relevant today, when U.S. politicians advocate stripping
homegrown terrorists of their nationality, and when Western countries like
the U.K. actually do so with complete impunity.

"Should citizenship be for sale?" European Union Democracy Observatory
on Citizenship (http://eudo-citizenship.eu/commentaries/citizenship-
forum/990-should-citizenship-be-for-sale). This debate, published by a
European think tank, came about as a result of the European Commission's
talks on Malta's citizenship-by-investment program and the tremendous
amount of controversy it provoked around the world. It gives an excellent
overview of the ethical, political, and legal issues that we ought to consider
when talking about whether citizenship should be bought and sold.

162   ENDNOTES

19 **The country was negotiating with the International Monetary Fund and the World Bank:** "The Union of the Comoros: Country Poverty Assessment—Brief," Islamic Solidarity Fund for Development. http://isfd.isdb.org/EN/publications/Documents/Other%20Publications/Comoros%20Country%20Poverty%20Assessment%20Brief.pdf

19 **only 60 percent of residents in Grande Comore, the biggest island, have access to electricity at all:** "Energy Sector Support Project: Union of the Comoros," African Development Bank Group. http://www.afdb.org/fileadmin/uploads/afdb/Documents/Project-and-Operations/Comoros%20-%20Energy%20Sector%20Support%20Project%20-%20Appraisal%20Report.pdf

22 **series of around twenty post-independence coups d'état:** "Revolution! Another coup in the world's most unstable country," by Claire Soares, *The Independent*, March 26, 2008. http://www.independent.co.uk/news/world/africa/revolution-another-coup-in-the-worlds-most-unstable-country-800608.html

27 **comparisons in a German magazine to Rupert Murdoch:** "Rupert Murdoch of the Comoros," by Clemens Recker, *Zenith Business Report*, issue 2, 2011. http://www.zenithonline.de/fileadmin/downloads/BusinessReport_abo_english/zBusinessReport_02_11_EN_web.pdf

27 **a member of Syrian President Bashar al-Assad's inner circle:** "Syria: Issues for the 112th Congress and Background on U.S. Sanctions," by Jeremy M. Sharp, Congressional Research Service. http://fpc.state.gov/documents/organization/167964.pdf

29 **"The corsairs in France would receive written permission from the king to attack foreign ships":** "Bob Denard, Hired Gun for Coups, Is Dead at 78," by Marlise Simons, *New York Times*, Oct. 16, 2007. http://www.nytimes.com/2007/10/16/world/europe/16denard.html?_r=0

42 **human rights organiz-ations had issued tersely worded recommendations:** "Without Citizenship: Statelessness, discrimination and repression in Kuwait," Refugees International and Open Society Justice Initiative. http://refugeesinternational.org/policy/in-depth-report/kuwait-without-citizenship

51 **there wasn't a strong, pre-existing sense of unifying Emirati nationalism:** "Nationalism in the Gulf States," by Neil Patrick,

October 2009, Kuwait Programme on Development, Governance and Globalisation in the Gulf States. http://eprints.lse.ac.uk/55257/1/Patrick_2009.pdf

55   **fewer than 5,000** *bidoon*: "Arab Spring energises Gulf's stateless," by Rania El Gamal and Sylvia Westall, Reuters, Dec. 19, 2012. http://www.reuters.com/article/2012/12/19/gulf-stateless-idUSL5E8NDAGU20121219

56   **a stateless man doused himself in gasoline:** "Immolation in Riyadh exposes plight of Arab stateless in Saudi Arabia," by Angus McDowall, Reuters, June 26, 2013. http://www.reuters.com/article/2013/06/26/us-saudi-immolation-poverty-idUSBRE95P0RX20130626

57   **Emirati citizens receive benefits that would make a Scandinavian social democracy blush:** "U.A.E.'s Drive for Emirati-Run Economy Is Thwarted by Handouts," by Matthew Brown, Bloomberg, Oct. 3, 2007. http://www.bloomberg.com/apps/news?pid=newsarchive&sid=axmdijbZMi5k

58   **2009 U.S. diplomatic cable:** "Kuwait's Stateless Bidoon: Background and Recent Promising Developments," WikiLeaks, June 3, 2009. https://www.wikileaks.org/plusd/cables/09KUWAIT558_a.html

59   **According to a 1995 Human Rights Watch report:** "The Bedoons of Kuwait: Citizens Without Citizenship," Human Rights Watch, August 1995. http://www.hrw.org/reports/1995/Kuwait.htm

59   **25 percent of Kuwait's army of 20,000 were** *bidoon*: ibid.

62   **"traitor without a nation":** "Arrested UAE Blogger Accused of Possessing Alcohol," Reuters, April 12, 2011. http://www.reuters.com/article/2011/04/12/us-emirates-activists-idUSTRE73B2EP20110412

63   **"waving the country's flag and clutching pictures of the Emir":** "Kuwait's Stateless Bidun Demand Greater Rights," by Simon Atkinson, *BBC News*, July 19, 2011. http://www.bbc.com/news/business-14185365

63   **dispensing cash bonuses:** "The 'Arab Spring' in the Kingdoms," by Zoltan Barany, Arab Center for Research and Policy Studies, Sept. 2012. http://english.dohainstitute.org/file/get/e02ce87b-f3ab-45d3-bfd8-3f3e97f6a6a9.pdf

63   **life was good for Emirati citizens:** "Why the Arab Spring Never Came to the U.A.E.," by Angela Shah, Time, July 18, 2011. http://content.time.com/time/world/article/0,8599,2083768,00.html

64   **stage of the Edinburgh festival:** "Comedians and Writers Lead Amnesty Campaign to Free Jailed UAE Activists," by Severin

164   Carrell, *The Guardian*, August 7, 2011. http://www.theguardian.com/culture/2011/aug/07/amnesty-uae-activists-edinburgh-festival?INTCMP=SRCH

71   the best country on the planet in which to be born: "Birth Right," *The Economist*, Jan. 1, 2013. http://www.economist.com/blogs/graphicdetail/2013/01/daily-chart?fsrc=scn/tw/te/bl/ed/birthright

71   travel visa-free to 170 countries out of a possible 196: "The Henley & Partners Visa Restrictions Index 2014," https://www.henleyglobal.com/files/download/hvri/HP%20Visa%20Restrictions%20Index%20141101.pdf

72   reads a Henley brochure: "Residence and Citizenship Practice Group," https://www.henleyglobal.com/residence-citizenship-practice-group/

80   by 2014, it hit 25 percent, with almost half of that amount coming from SIDF contributions: "Too Much of a Good Thing? Prudent Management of Inflows Under Economic Citizenship Programs," by Xin Xu, Ahmed El-Ashram and Judith Gold, International Monetary Fund, May 2015. http://www.imf.org/external/pubs/ft/wp/2015/wp1593.pdf

82   taken note of the country's progress: ibid.

84   investor-citizens spent $2 billion buying passports in 2014: "This Swiss Lawyer Is Helping Governments Get Rich Off Selling Passports," by Jason Clenfield, *Bloomberg Markets*, April 2015. http://www.bloomberg.com/news/articles/2015-03-11/passport-king-christian-kalin-helps-nations-sell-citizenship

87-88   "They come twice, once to get a residency card and once to get a passport": "Malta Offers Citizenship and All Its Perks for a Price," by Jenny Anderson, *New York Times*, April 30, 2015. http://www.nytimes.com/2015/05/01/business/dealbook/malta-offers-citizenship-and-all-its-perks-for-a-price.html

91   publish a ranking: "The Passport Index," Arton Capital, March 17, 2015. http://www.artoncapital.com/news/passport-index/

101   who was once stateless: *The Collected Papers of Albert Einstein, Volume 1: The Early Years, 1879–1902*, by Albert Einstein, Anna Beck, Peter Havas (Princeton University Press, 1987)

113   waiting list for renunciation interviews at embassies abroad: "Want to Shed U.S. citizenship? Get in Line," by Patrick Cain, *Global News*, August 21, 2014. http://globalnews.ca/news/1519628/want-to-shed-u-s-citizenship-get-in-line/

114 **an "exit tax":** Expatriation Tax, Internal Revenue Service. http://www.irs.gov/Individuals/International-Taxpayers/Expatriation-Tax

122 **donors at the conference promised $540 million in aid:** "Staff Report for the 2010 Article IV Consultation and Second Review Under the Extended Credit Facility," International Monetary Fund, March 2011. http://www.imf.org/external/pubs/ft/scr/2011/cr1172.pdf

123 **was just $387 million:** Comoros, United Nations Statistics Division. https://data.un.org/CountryProfile.aspx?crName=Comoros

126 **The AFDB puts revenues at 5.6 percent of GDP:** Energy Sector Reform Support Programme, Union of the Comoros, African Development Bank Group, Oct. 2014. http://www.afdb.org/fileadmin/uploads/afdb/Documents/Project-and-Operations/Comoros_-_Approved-_Energy_Sector_Reform_Support_Programme_-_PARSE_-_11_2014.pdf

126 **The IMF estimates the money came closer to 7.6 percent of GDP:** "Union of the Comoros: Letter of Intent, Memorandum of Economic and Financial Policies, and Technical Memorandum of Understanding," International Monetary Fund, May 18. 2013. http://www.imf.org/external/np/loi/2013/com/051813.pdf

126 **The World Bank wrote in an annual report:** Program Document, The World Bank, March 27, 2014. http://www-wds.worldbank.org/external/default/WDSContentServer/WDSP/IB/2014/04/10/000333037_20140410121708/Rendered/PDF/816710PGD0P131010Box38517 7B00OUO090.pdf

134 **Libya contributed security:** "Comoros: External Involvement in a Small Island State," by Simon Massey and Bruce Baker, Chatham House, July 2009. http://www.operationspaix.net/DATA/DOCUMENT/6286~v~Comoros___External_Involvement_in_a_Small_Island_State.pdf

134 **Libya donated 700,000:** "The Union of the Comoros: Country Poverty Assessment—Brief," Islamic Solidarity Fund for Development. http://isfd.isdb.org/EN/publications/Documents/Other%20Publications/Comoros%20Country%20Poverty %20Assessment%20Brief.pdf

134 **built a school block:** "Libya builds school block for University of Comoros," *The Tripoli Post*, Aug. 30, 2009. http://www.tripolipost.com/articledetail.asp?c=1&i=3524

145 **dozens of *bidoon* were fired:** "Rallying on Behalf of People Without Passports," by Sumaya Bakhsh, BBC News, June 5, 2015. http://www.bbc.com/news/blogs-trending-33008093

166   146   **"indicated that they were optimistic that a new ECP program with Kuwait would be agreed"**: "Union of the Comoros: Staff Report for the 2014 Article IV Consultation," International Monetary Fund, Jan.13, 2015. http://www.imf.org/external/pubs/ft/scr/2015/cr1534.pdf

Columbia Global Reports is a publishing imprint from Columbia University that commissions authors to do original on-site reporting around the globe on a wide range of issues. The resulting novella-length books offer new ways to look at and understand the world that can be read in a few hours. Most readers are curious and busy. Our books are for them.

ALSO IN FALL 2015
Shaky Ground:
The Strange Saga of the U.S. Mortgage Giants
Bethany McLean

Little Rice:
Smartphones, Xiaomi, and the Chinese Dream
Clay Shirky

www.globalreports.columbia.edu